"DRESS *and* UNDRESS"

A history of women's underwear

ELIZABETH EWING

Drama Book Specialists (Publishers)
New York

To Nicky

.

First published 1978
Copyright Elizabeth Ewing 1978

Printed in Great Britain

Drama Book Specialists (Publishers)
150 West 52nd Street
New York, New York 10019

Library of Congress Cataloging in Publication Data
Ewing, Elizabeth.
  Dress and undress.

  1. Underwear—History.   2. Lingerie—History.
I. Title.
GT2073.E89   391'.42   78–16819
ISBN 0-89676-000-6

Contents

Acknowledgments

This study of women's underwear of all kinds, considered as part of fashion history and of social history, derives from my earlier book *Fashion in Underwear*, now out of print. For additional information and access to information, illustrations and actual garments, past and present, I am greatly indebted to the staffs of the Fawcett Library, the London College of Fashion Library, the Museum of Costume, Bath and the Research Centre there, the Ruislip and Uxbridge Libraries, and the Victoria and Albert Museum Library, Photographic Library and Department of Textiles.

Valuable guidance on recent developments and trends has generously been given by Betty Williams, head designer of Berlei (UK), Gordon Murray of Chilprufe, Henry King of Du Pont (UK), Moira Keast of Kayser Bondor, Maureen Barnes of Marks and Spencer, Monty Skov of Metric Products of Reutingen, West Germany and Sue Loder of Triumph International.

The line drawings, by Jean Webber, were made from actual garments or contemporary illustrations.

List of Illustrations

I

Shaping up to Fashion – the Start of Underwear 3000 BC to AD 1350

When Christian Dior, king of couture in the years after the Second World War, said: 'Without foundations there can be no fashion', he could equally aptly have reversed the statement to: 'Without fashion there can be no foundations'. Fashion is a shape, a changing shape, and that shape was for centuries mainly, and sometimes even wholly, formed and controlled by what was worn underneath it, by the corset and other underwear. It was still so in Dior's day.

These underpinnings, so many and so varied, sometimes ephemeral but more often with a long and continuous history of their own, started at times as outerwear and then went underneath, usually because of their becoming more functional. On other occasions underwear, concealed or glimpsed for long periods, emerged as outerwear, provocative or glamorous in its own right. But in general it has its own story. That story and the story of outer fashion have for many centuries past been inseparable. Underwear existed in some form before fashion began, but it did not acquire any significance or any history until the dawn of fashion.

It might be assumed and is often accepted that the story of clothes and the story of fashion are the same, but this is not so. Fashion in clothes is a freak among the arts in that its existence as we understand it is limited to the Western World and to the period from the later Middle Ages onwards. Mankind has for innumerable centuries been drawing, painting, carving and sculpting, building, telling stories, dancing, singing songs and making music – in all sorts of ways such as these expressing himself and adjusting himself to the world around him by that exercise and projection of his feelings, thoughts and aspirations which we define in general as the arts.

But while these arts were continually changing and developing and taking on different forms from one era and one part of the world to another, men and women dressed in very much the same way gener-

1 Straight-falling Egyptian tunic with crossed shoulder band and knotted sash, *c*.1125 BC

ation after generation, century after century, even in one civilisation after another.

The history of clothing is usually, and reasonably, regarded by most people as dating from the time when mankind discovered how to spin and weave and therefore how to make fabrics that were durable and washable. This was many thousands of years ago, and the materials used were wool, flax or cotton, according to the part of the world concerned. In China from early days it was silk; the process of manufacture was until only a few centuries ago cherished as a closely guarded secret by that country.

It is impossible to say for certain which clothing material came first and from where, or how the method was first discovered of how to twist the raw materials together so as to produce continuous threads from which cloth could be woven by criss-crossing them at right angles on an elementary loom. But having produced lengths of fabric, people, men and women alike, draped them around their bodies in various ways and went on doing so.

The first continuous record of such clothes came from ancient Egypt from about 3000 BC, where, as would be expected, there was a considerable degree of sophistication in the draping. Sometimes we find narrow tunics, starting below the chest, extending to the ankles and often supported by a crosswise shoulder strap. Sometimes the drapery was drawn round the figure to the front, so as to mould it, and often a short semi-circular shoulder cape was also worn. So were loin cloths. In general, clothing was a status symbol: the higher the rank the more elaborate the clothing, while slaves and servants went naked or simply wore loin cloths. But there is no evidence of basic changes in style: similar ways of dressing remained. On the other hand, there was immense diversity and infinite dazzling elaboration in jewellery, accessories and all kinds of adornments, as every collection of Egyptian antiquities shows.

Sometimes in Egypt there was more than one layer of clothing, one opaque and one transparent. In this case the top one was transparent, but neither could be designated as being an under-garment as we understand the word. As a variation the clothing material, instead of simply being draped, was folded in two from end to end, with a hole or slit at the top for the head, so that it became more like a tunic. Pieces were also cut out down the sides, forming a letter 'T' and creating wide or narrow sleeves.

This general pattern of dress was to be continued and repeated, with variations in ways of folding and draping, through subsequent eras, including both Greek and Roman civilisations. It persists to this day in many parts of the world, notably in Indian saris, Arab and other Oriental robes, and can also be seen in the context of Chinese dress and

2 T-shaped tunic, Egypt, *c*.1500 BC

the Japanese kimono. There was nothing of recognisable fashion in it in the modern sense. There was no basic distinction between what men and women wore or between outerwear and underwear.

Strangely, however, from this early era there remain a few female terra cotta figures and figurines of two types separated from each other by about a thousand years of history and many hundreds of miles, but standing out from the mists of time as a starting point for underclothing and, in one type, specifically women's underclothing.

One outstanding example of the first type of figures is a Babylonian girl of about 3000 BC from Sumeria who wears what today would immediately be described as briefs. The other type comes from the Palace of Knossos, Crete, and is attired in the first recorded corset and crinoline. Her place in history is about 2000 BC. Both are unconcernedly bare-breasted and dressed in what in their day was obviously outerwear. An example of the first type can be seen in the Louvre, and of the other in the British Museum.

The briefs probably derived from the loin cloth, the most elementary of early and primitive garments for both sexes and one familiar in immensely scattered parts of the world from days as remote as those of cave drawings. Drawn up between the legs it becomes crude briefs, as is shown by other figures in later bas reliefs and vase drawings from many parts of the world. It is the oldest and the latest undergarment.

The Cretan figures, on the other hand, are far more intriguing in that they show a kind of dressing that is completely out of context with the traceable course of the history of clothes. Nothing remotely resembling them had been recorded from the ancient world until that brilliant but somewhat wayward archaeologist, Sir Arthur Evans, started his momentous excavations in Crete in the last years of the nineteenth century. There he found overwhelming evidence of a highly developed culture of 3000–1500 BC, similar to what Heinrich Schliemann had discovered at Troy and Mycenae some thirty years before. He not only shook the world of archaeology but also, incidentally, contributed something to the lesser matter of the accepted view of the history of clothes throughout the ages.

The significance of these long-lost ladies is that they show, very early and by an accident of survival and a trick of time, what was to happen aeons later in the Western World. But between them and the valid history of fashion and underwear is another chasm in time and space. The corseted figures in particular can only baffle and tease one out of thought.

When, several hundreds of years later, the era began that was to culminate in classical Greece, men and women alike were still wearing clothes formed of draped and folded lengths of material – the familiar classical draperies seen in great variety in the wealth of Greek sculp-

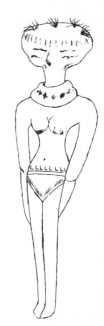

3 Sumerian terra cotta figure, *c.*3000 BC

4 Cretan snake goddess, *c.*2000 BC

5   Ionic chiton, 5th century BC – 2nd century AD

ture, frescoes and vases that remain. They are shown with a detail and naturalness absent from the formalised and geometric lines of Egyptian art.

In classical Greece, as in Egypt, there were frequently two layers of clothing, worn similarly by men and women alike, but neither ranked as underwear, though they pin-pointed its origin. The chiton or tunic was knee-length or full-length. It was either draped round the body and over one or both shoulders or else held on the shoulders by brooches or pins. Women often chose the latter more elegant effects, and both men and women sometimes added a belt to hold the tunic in at the waist. Sometimes there were also crossed bands that went over the shoulders and across the chest. A famous, very clear and simple example is the statue of the charioteer at Delphi.

Over the chiton went, when needed for warmth, a himation or cloak, similar in shape to the chiton and usually wrapped round the body, over the shoulders and sometimes also over the head. It varied in size. Sometimes it was the only garment worn by men, especially older men, who wore it draped round the waist and over the left shoulder, so that part of the upper body was bare. A smaller, shorter cloak was often

6 *(left)*   Doric chiton: Caryatid from the Erechtheum, Athens, about 420 BC

7 *(right)*   Statuette from Verona 50 BC–AD 50, imitating archaic Greek sculpture

8   The first modern bra and briefs. From the Villa Armerina, Sicily, a mosaic of the 4th century AD

worn but mainly by soldiers and horsemen. It was called a chlamys. Female statues show no trace of anything being worn under the chiton, but there is literary evidence that the Greeks, innovators in so many spheres of human progress, also set a lead in the relatively small matter of women's underwear and figure control. A band of linen or kid was bound round the waist and lower torso to shape and control it. It was known as the zoné, or girdle, and is referred to in the Odyssey and Iliad and also by Herodotus and others. Other Greek words were also apparently descriptive of breast bands, but exactly what this implied is not clear. The apodesmos, meaning a band, breast-band or girdle, occurs in a fragment of Aristophanes and also, some five hundred years later, in the Hellenistic writer Lucian.

A similar band, called the mastodeton, or breast band, was also worn round the bust, apparently to flatten or minimise it, as in the 1920s, and not, as in more recent history, to stress its curves. Occasionally the word mastodesmos occurs with a similar meaning. But none of the records help us to establish the extent to which such bands were worn by Greek women.

At any rate the Greeks can probably be given credit for introducing, or at least presaging, the most significant items of female underclothing, the corset and the brassière – the ones that were, many

9   Virgin and child. Byzantine ivory, late 11th or 12th century

centuries later, to have more influence than any others on fashion, when this came into existence.

Clothing in ancient Rome followed closely on the lines of that in Greece and elsewhere. In Rome, too, women sometimes wore bands of material round the hips and bust – a cestus or girdle is referred to by the poet Martial and seems to have been similar to the zoné, but wider, and the strophium, or breast band, is mentioned by Cicero. A relief shows Cleopatra wearing a wide shaped band at her waist. A Roman mosaic in the Imperial Villa, Piazza Armerina in Sicily, shows female athletes wearing a bikini – briefs and bra – in the fourth century AD.

There is evidence that in the days of the grandeur that was Rome clothes became more ostentatious than ever before and that women wore elaborate layers of clothing, mainly as a sign of rank and importance. Some of this may have been regarded as underwear, but it is impossible to be certain and in view of the loosely draped clothing it would not be likely to have a shape and character of its own.

From these early times onwards for many centuries one is confronted with the difficulty that underwear would not be seen. While statues, vases and frescoes show some of the richness and colourfulness, the inventive patterns, designs and embroideries that decorated clothing, and while the profusion of jewellery, beads, buckles and similar adornments worn can still be seen in surviving antiquities, of underwear there is no trace. All that can be said is that in country after country, century after century, similar draped lengths of material continued to constitute clothing. Tanagra statuettes of women of the first century AD vary scarcely at all from those of fifth-century BC Greece.

When, in the fourth century AD, the capital of the Roman Empire was transferred to the site of the ancient Byzantium, which became Constantinople, the Eastern influence led to the first significant change in clothing that was to influence the Western World. For the first time trousers were worn. To start with they were, as previously in the East, regarded as mainly women's wear and unmanly. Over them went tunics of varying lengths, and at times men too wore such trousers in a knee-length style under their tunics or draped clothes. Their derivation is usually regarded as Persian and they were the precursors of all subsequent trousers and other two-legged garments worn as outerwear or underwear by both sexes. In mosaics in Byzantine churches Emperors are shown wearing knee-length tunics with long narrow sleeves, long loose cloaks and occasionally with accompanying 'barbarian' trousers.

In Northern Europe the Saxons and Celts wore these trousers, and from the Bronze Age onwards loose tunics or draped lengths of material were also worn there, as over most of the world.

When, in the later Middle Ages, the recorded history of clothing in

Britain began to take a coherent form by means of illuminated manuscripts which are still extant, men and women were, as all over the world, still wearing loose tunics and cloaks of the familiar pattern, and trousers of some sort were also seen, usually on men.

10   Medieval loose robes. St Dorothy and the Infant Christ, by Francesco di Giorgio, 1682 (Reproduced by courtesy of the Trustees, The National Gallery, London)

From all these centuries there were therefore to emerge, as items of underwear, the man's shirt and woman's shift, both derived from the tunic, and also what would, much later, become respectively trousers, underpants and women's drawers, later called knickers – all originating in the early trousers. As with subsequent articles of underwear all these started as outer garments.

The beginning of fashion and of the intricate and continually varying undergarments that were to serve the main purpose of the shape-making of which fashion was chiefly to consist came suddenly in England and in Western Europe generally at the middle of the twelfth century. This was when, for the first time since the statues from Crete produced a fashion enigma, women began to wear clothing fitted closely to their bodies.

The woman's long, loose tunic-style dress began about 1150 to be drawn close to the figure by means of lacing at the back, sides or front, so that it became tight-fitting and waisted. There was as yet no cutting to form the waist and no separation of bodice and skirt, but the lacing created the first closely defined waistline in modern dress history. Buttons and other fastenings did not yet exist, so lacing was the obvious way to achieve this effect.

Why there should have been such a breakaway from the age-long tradition of loose clothing at this particular juncture it is hard to say. The reason may be that the hold of the Church was weakening and the idea of romantic love, part of the new, more secular outlook, was encouraging women to reveal their physical and sexual attractions. Whether this was the case or not, the emergence of the waist was the start of fashion which, for centuries to come, was to consist of continually shaping and re-shaping the outward appearance of the human body, so as to make it express the feelings and attitudes of the individual to himself and the society in which he lived, and also to make use of ever-changing developments in textiles and in making-up processes.

It also provided the real beginning of the story of underwear. The prototype of the corset, the chief shapemaker, appears in a twelfth-century manuscript in the famous Cottonian collection, presented to the British nation by Sir John Cotton in 1700 and now in the British Museum. The collection includes medieval manuscripts and one of these shows the Devil, represented as a woman, as monastic illustrators were fond of doing. The figure, which has a human form but a grotesque, malevolent, birdlike head, outspread wings and webbed feet, wears a tight-fitting bodice extending from the shoulders to below the waist and closely laced up in the front, with a dangling lace falling below it almost to the ground. There is a strange tulip-shaped skirt, so long that it is knotted up in a big loop.

This is the earliest British record of the shapemaker that was to

11 'Fiend of Fashion'. 12th-century shaped, laced bodice, from Cottonian MS

become the corset, and it is momentous in underwear history for this reason. It is, however, evidently an outer garment and it was not until some three centuries later that similar items of wear were to become undergarments. This fact, however, in no way invalidates its importance as an innovation in the history of fashion and above all of underwear.

By the thirteenth century, however, women were again wearing long, loose shapeless dresses, pouched over a girdle at the waist, and with no figure definition at all. Again, it is impossible to reason or speculate why this happened.

In the mid-fourteenth century, the fitted, tightly waisted fashion came back, this time to stay. Men as well as women began to wear clothes that were shaped to the body and from now on there was to be no looking back to the centuries of universal loose drapery or softly falling shapeless robes until, perhaps, the caftans of the 1970s.

Shapes would come and shapes would go, but this was the real beginning of fashion. From now on fashion was established and it was to proceed on its way, continually shaping and re-shaping the human form in ways that, in retrospect, form a panorama that is often even more bewildering and more difficult to comprehend than are those millenia when the idea of creating clothes with a shape apparently was not visualised by anyone anywhere – except perhaps those ancient Cretans.

In the process of shaping, underclothes were to play a main part and would pass through changes as many and as bewildering as would fashion itself. Without them outer fashion would not have been able to exist at all. Underwear, moreover, would have its own fashions and at many times be as sophisticated as outer fashion. The two would also intermingle.

This, however, was for the future. At first the shape was the thing, and the undergarments that created it were to be primarily functional and usually carefully contrived. This in itself was, indeed, a step forward. In the Middle Ages, the religious idea had prevailed that the body was sinful and underwear therefore something rather shameful. The hair shirt was a garment of penance. People did penance and indicated their humility or shame by appearing in only their shirts or smocks (the early Saxon word for chemise) on pilgrimages or when craving the forgiveness of the Church. They therefore cannot have taken pride in their underwear.

Fashion was born as the Middle Ages ended but the centuries-old tradition of loose robes died hard. It persists to this day in ecclesiastical, legal, academic and other formalised or ceremonial clothing. It continued to be manifest for a century or two more in paintings and frescoes. Biblical and historical figures in European paintings by the great masters of the fifteenth and sixteenth centuries are continually shown wearing such robes. They are depicted with immense grandeur and often in gorgeous colourfulness in the works of Bellini, Titian, Veronese and Raphael, although some of these also show the new stiff, tight bodices that were the start of fashion.

Fashion, moreover, has remained to this day a Western monopoly. Elsewhere it has no appreciable existence except when and where the populace has been 'converted' to Western ways, thereby sharing in a wealth of new means of communication between nations. These links are particularly strong in the visual sphere.

2

From Willowy Waists to Flaring Farthingales 1350–1600

Almost all the historical developments in women's fashions have centred upon the waist and have usually been dictated by its being narrowed, lowered, raised or, for one or two brief periods, deliberately obliterated. In all the immense variety of shapes created in this way – mostly artificial and almost incredible today because they bore little or no resemblance to the natural female shape – the waist has been the pivot on which fashion has revolved. Underwear has very largely been dominated and conditioned by this fact.

The fashionable waist has rarely been entirely natural and some way of outlining or emphasising it has been in existence from the earliest days of fashion. In some early effigies on surviving monuments and brasses, dating from the fourteenth and fifteenth centuries, there seem to be signs that something like the Greek zoné and its variations in the ancient world was worn to cinch the waist.

From the fourteenth century the moulding of the waist, previously contrived, in its brief twelfth-century emergence, by drawing together and lacing up a naturally loose robe to the shape of the body, was achieved by cutting and sewing the outer garment to the appropriately waisted pattern, as has been done ever since. People at this time were learning how to shape clothes and skill in making-up was developing as the medieval local craft guilds became more organised and efficient. The biggest development in this respect came in the reign of Queen Elizabeth, when the vigorous driving force of Cecil and the Privy Council created something like a national policy of wages, prices, apprenticeship and conditions of work in the clothing, as in other trades.

Long before that time the bodices of women's dresses had become long and narrow and the dresses, instead of being all in one piece, were joined to a flowing skirt at the hips, where a decorative belt was worn in the fourteenth century. Buttons were invented at this time and are

12 Shaped bodice and narrow waist of 1375. Dame Margaret Cobham in a brass rubbing at Cobham, Kent

13   Slim elegance in another brass rubbing, of 1416, showing Sir Simon Felbrygge and his wife Margaret at Felbrigg Church, Norfolk

seen on many effigies, including that of Anne of Bohemia, wife of Richard II, in Westminster Abbey. They were not, however, used in underclothes until the seventeenth century, tapes and ribbons being employed there when fastenings were necessary.

Under the tight, elongated bodices there was worn, in addition to the traditional voluminous shift or smock, a stiffened linen underbodice. This was originally known as a 'cotte', an early French word used for any close-fitting garment and similar in meaning to *côte*, the word for ribs. As the cult of the slim figure progressed, this garment was made increasingly figure-defining and rigid by the use of paste as a stiffener between two layers of linen.

The 'cotte' thus became the earliest form of what we call the corset, and therefore one of the most important developments in the history of underwear. This stiffened bodice became known from the fifteenth century as a 'body' or 'pair of bodys', being made in two pieces fastened together at the back and front. From the seventeenth century the alternative words 'stays' and 'a pair of stays' came into current use. In French it was called, similarly, a '*corps*' or, in an earlier spelling, '*cors*'. It was at times a laced bodice, worn as an outer garment by women. It still survives in this form in the traditional national dress of many European countries. It has been suggested that the modern word corset was the result either of adding the diminutive '*et*' to '*cors*' or of linking '*serrer*', meaning to close tightly, to the word '*cors*'. The 'body' became more recognisably the forerunner of the corset when, in the sixteenth century, it began to be fortified with whalebone. It was the usual foundation of the increasingly rigid, elongated outer bodices that

14   The corset as an outer garment in a painting, *An Allegory of Fame,* by Bernardo Strozzi (1581–1644) (Reproduced by courtesy of The Trustees, The National Gallery, London)

characterised fashion then and in the following centuries, and it kept such bodices geometrically straight-lined. It made their severe shape possible. Sometimes the whalebone bodice was itself an outer garment, made of appropriately rich materials. Examples of this emergence of an inner garment as an outer one were a recurrent feature of fashion history and some actual garments of this kind have survived from the eighteenth century and are preserved in costume collections. Apparently, however, the corset was not invariably worn even by early Elizabethan women. Stubbs in his *Anatomy of Abuses* (1585) says: 'Women have doublets and jerkins as the men have'. Not till the middle of the reign did there come a great change, when, he adds, 'the body was imprisoned in whalebone to the hips'.

Various references to the corset by name occur in surviving records from the thirteenth century onwards. It was for long taken for granted that this garment was what we call the corset, but within the past century increasing doubts and denials have been voiced on this subject by costume experts. It now appears that earlier writers on costume had confused the medieval Latin word 'corsettus' with their own term corset – a confusion which on the surface is supported by references in medieval literature to the smallness of ladies' waists.

The error was possibly started by Joseph Strutt, one of the earliest writers on medieval life, who wrote in the mid-eighteenth century: 'Towards the conclusion of the fourteenth century, the women were pleased with the appearance of a long waist; and in order to produce that effect, they invented a strange disguisement called a corse or corset'. This was accepted and it took a long time to unmask his own 'strange disguisement' in the use of the word.

Many early records point to a quite different garment under the name of a corset and they all indicate an outer garment. The household accounts book of Eleanor, Countess of Leicester, for the date 25 May 1265, contains an item: 'For 9 ells, Paris measure, for summer robes, corsets and cloaks for the same . . . Richard, King of the Normans and Edward his son'. Corsets in this context seem quite out of place. In 1299 a wardrobe account of Edward I refers to a corset of miniver, which is squirrel fur and therefore even less apt. A manuscript of about 1530 described 'her seneschal . . . mounted on a great courser, and in a rich corset of grene, girt wit a white silken lace'. Again the description is wide of the mark – a corset would not be visible.

Dr Joan Evans, an outstanding authority on the Middle Ages, concluded after close study of the subject that the early 'corset' was 'a cloak of oval cut varying in length'. This seems to fit the available evidence. A similar view is voiced by Kay Staniland in a detailed account of the problem of the early corset. She subscribes to the view that the stays/corset developed from the stiffened 'body' or bodice of the sixteenth century, but she believes that the medieval 'corsettus' was something quite different. First applied to men's garments, in the thirteenth century, and in the fourteenth to those of women, it is, she says, usually one of several garments forming a 'robe' – tunic, supertunic, cloak or mantle and/or corsettus, all made from the same material. These materials varied from thick woollens to the richest of embroidered silks and velvets, lined with wool or more often, fur.

Drs C. Willett and Phillis Cunnington, differentiate between the early and the later corset, but describe the earlier one as a close-fitting bodice and record that the word 'corset' began to be used as a refinement for stays at the close of the eighteenth century. Other evidence confirms this: *The Times* of 24 June 1795 said that 'corsettes about six inches long, and a slight buffon tucker of two inches high, are now the only defensive paraphernalia of our fashionable Belle'. In the next year the specifications of a patent referred to 'an improvement in the making of stays and corsettes'. From then on corset was an accepted term.

Important as this distinction about the corset is, because of its effect on much-quoted early allusions to the garment, it does not change the actual course of fashion or the story of underwear. The first dominant fashion trend was the narrow waist and the first significant article of underwear, as opposed to the timeless shift or smock, was the stiffened bodice. An early poem says, in obvious praise:

> *The lady was clad in purple pall*
> *With gentill body and middle small.*

Chaucer writes of ladies of quality in his time, the late fourteenth century, as 'clad in rich kirtle, their bodies being long and small'. The poet Gower at the same period gives a similar picture of the admired female figure:

> *He seeth her shape forthwith, all*
> *Her body round, her middle small.*

Dunbar, the Scottish poet, in *The Thistle and the Rose*, says of some beauties that 'their middles were as small as wands'. Leonardo da Vinci wrote less poetically that people were suffocated by their corsets.

Under these narrow bodices with their slim waists the shift or smock was at first the only known item of underwear. Loose, wide, long-sleeved and ankle-length, and made of linen or cotton in its original guise, it remained so for centuries, even though the outer fashionable shape became closely defined at the waist. But Chaucer in the *Romaunt of the Rose*, written about 1370, says:

> *. . . through her smocke yurought with silke*
> *The fleshe was sene as white as milke.*

This makes it evident that even in early times very fine materials were sometimes used for the smock.

Together with the narrower bodice and the 'cotte' or 'body' worn under it, but over the smock, came an increasing width in skirts. This tendency continued steadily from the fourteenth century through Tudor times. Under the wider skirts petticoats were worn. Exactly when this became customary is not known. J.R. Planché in his *History of British Costume* (1834) points out that an early portrait of Queen Elizabeth shows her with her 'upper dress being a sort of coat of black velvet and ermine, fastened only on the clasp and flying open below, disclosing the waistcoat and kirtle or petticoat of white silk or silver embroidered with black'. Such open skirts, revealing rich petticoats, had been worn since the time of Henry VIII.

Certain early manuscripts and paintings, of the late fourteenth and the fifteenth centuries, show skirts held up and evident petticoats appearing underneath them. Fastened round the waist with tapes or ribbons, these petticoats became something of a status symbol, the number worn being evidence of rank or wealth or awareness of fashion. The petticoats were of wool, linen or cotton and often coloured. There are early references to red being used, so that the famous 'red flannel petticoat' of Victorian days has a very long pedigree.

In addition to petticoats there was, however, also the kirtle. This was

15   Fur-trimmed dress looped up to show petticoat, *c.*1450

L'angloyfe.

Ainfi veftue eft vne femme Angloife
Par le deffus fon bonnet eft fourré,
On la cognoiſt (bié qu'aux lieux on ne voi
Facilement à fon bonnet carré.   fe)

16 *(left)*   Fashion picture of 1567 from Paris, showing petticoat

17 *(right)*   Lady Jane Grey in a full-skirted dress, opening to reveal an elaborate petticoat all down the front. Portrait *c.*1547 attributed to Master John

described by Stubbs who, in an account quoted by Planché, says that the petticoats of fashionable women of the time, the late sixteenth century, are 'of the best cloth and the finest dye, and even of silk, grograin, &c, fringed about the skirts with silk of a changeable colour. But what is more vain, of whatever the petticoat be, yet must they have kirtles, for so they call them, of silk, velvet, grograin, tafftee, satin, or scarlet, bordered with gard, lace, fringe, and I cannot tell what'. Therefore, concludes Planché, the kirtle was 'distinguished from the gown and petticoat, and is the garment worn immediately under the gown and at this time completely discovered by it, the skirt or train of the gown or robe being only just visible on each side of the figure'. The visible petticoat was to recur frequently in fashion from this time onwards, bringing glamour and sex appeal to underwear whenever it did so. Such petticoats were sometimes quilted, for warmth and to show off fashionable full skirts.

Skirts became fuller from the end of the fifteenth century. Clothes were also gradually being made of richer and richer materials. This was due mainly to the rise in trade and to the pouring into Western Europe of the rich culture of the Byzantine and post-classical world, which followed the fall of Constantinople in 1453. Among the new imports were luxury fabrics of great stiffness and richness, which were used for clothes. These obviously could not be shown to effect in the clinging, softly falling styles used for clothes made of the earlier native woollens.

The art of wearing gorgeous silks, satins, damasks, velvets and brocades to full effect was first manifest in Spain and Italy. These countries were the spearhead of the Renaissance and the fashions started there caused a revolution in dress which soon spread widely through Western Europe. The sumptuous materials were stiff and weighty. They had to stand out firmly and grandly, so the human frame became a kind of mobile scaffolding to support the splendour which the Elizabethans loved in dress, as in other aspects of their exuberant life.

The chief device used to achieve this effect transformed skirts. The full bell-shaped Tudor ones, held out by petticoats and kirtle, were not enough for the Elizabethans, whose lives were an extravaganza of creative energy and vitality poured into whatever they did, whether it was exploration, literature, drama, art or zestful, rumbustious living. Fashion, both for men and women, went to wild extremes and decreed that both sexes should look twice as large as nature made them.

By the 1550s, in the reign of Mary Tudor, who had married Philip II of Spain in 1554, skirts began to be made enormous by being artificially supported from underneath by the farthingale. The farthingale is said to have come from Spain, which is likely, not only because of the

18   Mid-16th-century dress showing Spanish farthingale

Royal link but also because that country was the most powerful in Western Europe, with dominions rapidly extending not only over its own native territory but also over Germany, the Netherlands, parts of Italy and the New World across the Atlantic. The word is a corruption of the Spanish word *verdugado*, derived from the word *verdugo*, stick, and meaning something distended by rods or hoops. It was spelt in various ways in England, where the first record of it dates to Bishop Latimer's Sermons of 1552, about the time of its first appearance.

First came the Spanish farthingale. It probably started as a petticoat 'boosted' by a series of graduated corded hoops, but soon the hoops were of cane, whalebone or wire. In its more modest manifestations the farthingale was almost a perfect replica of the Cretan lady's skirt of 3,500 years before, but it grew wider and wider, until, by the late 1550s, it was a separate framework over which the petticoats and skirt were draped.

19 French farthingale, *c.*1580

The farthingale was originally a Court fashion, contrived to display in full the splendour of the fabrics which were by then being used for clothes, but it spread to some extent elsewhere, although its vogue does not seem to have been so general as that of the eighteenth-century hoops and the nineteenth-century crinoline. In Elizabethan times the barrier between Court circles and the fashionable world on the one hand and the rest of the populace on the other was greater than in subsequent periods, and the peasant population, living on the land, was larger. One obviously could not work there in the panoply of a farthingale.

20 'Body' with steel bands and busk with long, tapering front, *c.*1580

The sizes of the farthingale became immense, as is recorded in Heywood's *Epigrams*, published in 1590:

> *Alas, poor verdingales must lie in the streete,*
> *To house them no doore in the citee made meete,*
> *Syns at our narrow doores they on can not win,*
> *Send them to Oxforde, at Brodegates to get in.*

During the late 1570s a new type of farthingale, known as the French one, was introduced, and was even more grotesque. It consisted of a kind of vast horizontal hoop worn at the waist, but tilted down at the front to accommodate the elongated front of the stiffened bodice. Over it were draped the petticoats, kirtles and skirts. The skirts of the French, 'drum' farthingale sometimes opened over rich petticoats, made of gorgeous materials and embroidered and elaborately trimmed with gimp, fringe and other embellishments. This is frequently seen in portraits of Queen Elizabeth and other fashionable ladies of the time. With the alternative Spanish or 'wheel' farthingale several linen petticoats, as well as the elaborate ones, were sometimes worn to give additional width to the skirt. The French farthingale is the most

21   Queen Elizabeth in a
French farthingale, *c.*1592

unnatural and probably the most uncomfortable and inconvenient
garment in the whole story of fashion. One recent writer has described
it as 'one of the most hideous distortions that has ever obsessed the
imagination and distorted the lines of the human body'. The two styles
of farthingale did not, however, disappear from fashion until about
1625.

For those Elizabethans who did not run to such extremes of fashion,
there was an alternative – a roll or 'sausage' of stiffened material worn
round the waist under the skirts, so as to hold them out to a lesser
degree. It was known as a 'bum roll' and was to recur in later fashion.

It was, however, not accepted as fashionable. A character in the Ben Jonson play, *The Poetaster*, is said to have 'debased' herself by changing from farthingale to bum roll.

In the late sixteenth century stiffened bodices of an increasingly formidable kind were also being worn, usually under the dress, but over the smock, sometimes as part of the dress. They were, however, still always known as a 'body' or 'pair of bodys'. Ben Jonson seems to refer to this garment when he writes, in about 1600, of

> *The whalebone man*
> *That quilts the bodies I have leave to span.*

The stiffened linen bodice, with whalebone or steel to give it extra rigidity, was also sometimes padded with wool. Next it was given a front 'busc' or busk.

The busk, credited with having had its origin in Italy and with having been brought to England by Catherine or Aragon, was another artificial support given to the figure. It was originally made of wood, horn, ivory, metal or whalebone, and was at times carved or painted. It was shaped rather like a long paper knife, thicker at the top than at the bottom, and could extend from above the bust to the waist or even nearly to the hips. It was slotted into the Elizabethan bodice or was part of the 'body', or early corset, and it was held in place with a lace, so that it could be pulled in or out. It is believed to have been produced on occasion to administer a sharp rap to an importunate male, just as the eighteenth-century fan was. The lace, like the eighteenth-century garter, was bestowed as a special favour on the man who had found favour with the lady to whom it belonged.

22   Early 17th-century 'bum roll', worn instead of the farthingale

The busk remained a feature of dress in many succeeding periods and it has continued to be an important component of 'stays' and corsets right up to the present century. It still exists in a few of the remaining very traditional corset designs. A collection of eighteenth-century busks is on view at the Castle Museum, York.

By the second half of the sixteenth century whalebone was also being used at the sides and back of the 'body' which was laced up the front. A stomacher, a stiffened strip of material reaching from bust to below waist, was worn behind the front lacing under the open-fronted dresses of the second half of the sixteenth century. As the Elizabethan fashion for very stiff, elongated bodices developed, with the front of the bodice extending to a point as low as was compatible with being able to sit down, the 'body' became even more severe, to give the required fashionable, almost tube-like straightness to the bodice of the dress. It was sometimes made of leather and whalebone, and as it encased the body from above the bust almost to the hips it must have been an instrument of near-torture.

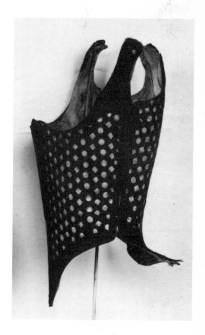

23   Iron corset of 16th century

Catherine de Medici, wife of Henry II of France (1579–1589), who was something of a fashion dictator in her time, is believed to have frowned on a thick waist as amounting to the height of bad manners and to have prescribed thirteen inches as the ideal. She is also said to have introduced a particularly rigid and powerful 'corps', hardened and stiffened and rising almost to the throat, so that the effect was to create almost a drainpipe shape.

Tradition has it that she was also the originator of the much-discussed iron corset of the time. This looked almost like a piece of armour, made in an openwork design over which silk or velvet could be stretched. It was hinged at one side and closed at the other with a hasp or pin. A few examples still exist. Some students of fashion believe it was worn as an outer garment, in addition to the accepted stiff 'body', but there is now also a more widely held view that it was a remedial or surgical type of garment and not one intended for ordinary wear. There is no evidence of the latter.

The stiffened 'body' as it actually existed was, however, formidable enough. It was satirically and scornfully described by Philip Gosson in 1591 in his 'Pleasant Quippes for Upstart Newfangled Gentlewomen':

> These privie coates by art made strong,
> With bones, with paste and suchlike ware,
> Whereby their backe and sides grew long
> And now they harnest gallants are;
> Were they for use against the foe,
> Our dames for Amazons might goe.

> But seeing they doe only stay
> The course that nature doth intend,
> And mothers often by them slay
> Their daughters yoong, and worke their end;
> What are they els but armours stout,
> Wherein like gyants Jove they flout?

Although, unlike the 'body' and the farthingale, it cannot be classified as an undergarment, the ruff, that other dominating feature of the Elizabethan lady's apparel, derives directly from underwear. Its origin lay in the edging of the shift, which was often visible at the neckline of dresses. Such an edging was frequently embroidered either in white or in black and examples of Elizabethan 'black embroidery' still exist, including one in the Victoria and Albert Museum. When lace was invented in the sixteenth century it was used at the neck of chemises showing above the top of dresses, and from this the ruff started about 1550 as a quite separate item of dress. To begin with it was small but its dimensions increased gradually.

Its vogue, for both men and women, was closely bound up with the introduction into England of starch. This was effected in 1564 by a Dutch woman, Madame Dingham Vander Plasse, and it made it possible to wear a deep ruff which would stand up by itself. In the grandiose Elizabethan manner the ruff could rise as high as the top of the wearer's head at the back. Stubbs writes scornfully: 'There is a certain liquid matter which they call starch, wherein the devil hath learned them to wash and dive their ruffs, which, being dry, will then stand stiff and inflexible about their necks'. He also says that the starch 'was made of wheat flour, bran, or other grains, sometimes of roots and other things, and of all colours and hues, such as white, red, blue, purple and the like'. The starched underwear worn by generations of girls and women to come was, unlike this, proudly white. Madame Vander Plasse, he adds, 'met with much encouragement amongst the nobility and gentry of this country, and was the first who publicly taught the art of starching, her price being four to five pounds for each scholar, and twenty shillings in addition for teaching them how to seethe or make the starch'.

24 The Elizabethan ruff, as shown by Nicholas Hilliard in *Portrait of an Unknown Woman*

Some ruffs were so vast that spoons were made with specially long handles to enable the wearers to eat. Unlike the farthingale, the ruff continued to be worn during a great part of the seventeenth century. It is seen in several portraits by Rembrandt, including two of Margaretta Tripp, one of which is dated 1663, and one of an eighty-three-year-old woman. Van Dyck (1599–1641) also testifies to the continued wearing of the ruff by showing it in his portraits.

Stockings are not usually included in underwear, although for centuries they were almost concealed, in the case of women at any rate, and therefore could claim to be 'underneaths'. Today we classify them rather as accessories, but their close connection with underwear and especially with the knitting associated with underwear earns reference to how and when they came into the fashion picture and how they changed and developed.

The origin of stockings is obscure, but from surviving records the salient fact emerges that 'socks, stockings and hosiery were the last of the articles of wearing apparel which man invented'. There are scattered references to the wearing of something like puttees – lengths of cloth wrapped round the legs – in Roman times, but before then no words, hieroglyphics or pictures in Hebrew, Greek or Egyptian record anything resembling stockings. A classical Latin word *fascia* seems to mean 'a bandaging or wrapping round the leg' for protection against the elements. The Romans may have adopted this from the Gauls, and they may also have brought it to Britain. Fascia were, however, regarded as suitable only for old men and women, and as effeminate. The Normans, famed for the richness of their dress, wore them, William Rufus being on record as wearing costly hose, still of cloth. There were sumptuary laws limiting the cost of stockings worn by servants and tradesmen and their wives and children in 1533 in the reign of Edward III, and in that of Mary Tudor in 1555. Tights were worn by men in many parts of Europe in the fourteenth, fifteenth and sixteenth centuries.

Women's legs were concealed, but the first record of their wearing stockings comes in an illustration in Queen Mary's Psalter in the Royal Collection in the British Museum. Ascribed to the reign of Edward II, who came to the throne in 1306, it shows a lady in her boudoir, seated on the edge of her bed and being handed a recognisable stocking by a servant. She wears the other stocking. They are shaped in the modern way. Chaucer's Wife of Bath is described as wearing stockings, and this would be in the latter part of the fourteenth century:

> *Her hosen were of fine scarlet redde,*
> *Full straite y-teyed.*

In the sixteenth century Rabelais, writing of the dress of the people of

Thélèmes, in *Gargantua*, described the women's stockings: 'The ladies . . . wore stockings of scarlet crimson, or ingrained purple dye, which reached just three inches above their knees, having a "list" beautified with exquisite embroideries, and rare incisions of the cutter's art'. A *list* was a strip of other material used as edging.

Queen Elizabeth in 1566 received 'a pair of black *knit* silk stockings for a new yeare's gift' from Mistress Montague, her silkwoman, who had knitted them herself. The event was considered important enough to be recorded by Stow, who also says that the Queen was greatly delighted and that the donor promised that 'I will presently set more in hande'. To which the Queen said: 'Do so, for indeed I like silke stockings so well, because they are pleasant, fine and delicate, and henceforth I will weare no more cloth stockings'. Thus began the love of silk stockings which was to be echoed by women for nearly 400 years, until nylon took over in the 1940s. Within about 12 years silk stockings had been wiped off the fashion map.

Stockings became an important item in the Elizabethan lady's dress, and were made of 'silk, jarnsey, worsted cruel, or of the finest yarn, thread or cloth that could possibly be had'. They were of all colours, were 'cunningly knit' and 'curiously indented in every point with quirks, clocks, open seams, and everything else accordingly'. Stockings were looked on as suitable presents. Lady Arbella Stuart, living at the court of James VI and I, presented Queen Anne with silk stockings as a gift calculated to win her favour with her kinswoman: 'I mean to give her majesty two pair of silk stockings lined with plush, and two pair of gloves lined', she wrote.

A few early stockings survive. There is at the Castle Museum in York a pair dated 1660, of gold silk with heavy silver embroidery on the front of the foot and lower leg. The Victoria and Albert Museum has a pair made of wool belonging to the seventeenth century.

Nottingham, as a great wool town, became an early centre of the hand-knitting industry. Near there, in Calverton, in 1589, William Lee, a poor parson, invented a machine for knitting stockings more quickly than by hand. After demonstrating his machine, with the aim of securing a patent for it, he presented Queen Elizabeth with a pair of silk stockings made on it. While she admired them, she was afraid of an invention which to her seemed likely to put people in the hand-knitting trade out of work. Disappointed over his failure to obtain a patent, Lee took his invention to France. After his death in 1610 his brother brought back a few of his machines to London and Nottingham and the frame-knitting trade was established in this way.

London and the South, being near to the Spitalfields silk market and situated at the hub of fashion, concentrated on the manufacture of silk stockings. In Nottingham trade, growing more slowly, was built up on the substantial worsted stockings produced from the long-fibred wool of Sherwood sheep. This trade spread throughout the seventeenth century. Hand-knitted and frame-knitted hosiery co-existed without the disruption Queen Elizabeth had feared, and hand-knitted goods were still a considerable export in the latter part of the eighteenth century.

The rather gradual development of the trade was due to the slowness of the process of yarn-spinning. It took eight spinners to keep one weaver at work. The speeding up of yarn production was the result of Hargreaves' invention, in 1764, of the spinning jenny, which meant that several spindles could operate on one spinning wheel, and of Arkwright's 1767 improvement on this. His great contribution was a machine which spun yarn by the roller method. Like a host of subsequent mechanical inventions in industry, both these achievements caused widespread labour troubles based on the recurrent fear of human labour being superseded. But they proved to be landmarks in the progress of textiles and clothing. The immense part taken by knitting machines in all the variety of underwear which was to be worn by the whole community in the nineteenth and twentieth centuries had its origin in that sixteenth-century stocking machine of William Lee.

Night clothes did not have any identity of their own until the eighteenth century. Up to the sixteenth century most people seem to have slept naked, but some early illustrations show sick people and mothers of new-born children in bed, wearing some sort of garment. This was probably a version of the daytime shirt or smock and it was increasingly worn at night from the sixteenth to the eighteenth century, when it began to be known by name and acquired a category of its own in lists of garments. It became longer in the case of women, but remained full and straight and was usually made of the white cotton general for most people's underwear. It followed the smock in being at times trimmed with lace or embroidery or rows of tucks. It did not move into anything like glamour until the rest of women's underwear did this in the late 1880s. Men's nightshirts likewise followed the lines of day shirts. Nightcaps were generally worn by both sexes, following the daytime custom of the covered head which was general throughout the Elizabethan period.

The Lady Anne Clifford, in 1617, said in her diary: 'I went to church in my rich night gown and petticoat'. She obviously was using the word in a sense then accepted – an informal day dress.

3

The Tempestuous Petticoat
1600–1680

The Elizabethan style of dress lasted with all its exaggeration, splendour and rigidity for many years after the death of the Queen. Huge farthingales and long, stiff corset-like bodices continued to be the fashion until about 1625. The new Queen, Anne of Denmark, had a more than Elizabethan love of pomp and circumstance in dress, of rich, exotic, extravagantly be-jewelled garments and of the farthingale which set them off so grandly. She amassed a fabulous collection of jewellery. All this was built up to new heights by her obsessive enthusiasm for elaborate masques, plays, pageants and dancing, all gorgeously spectacular, which dominated the life of her Court throughout her life. For these the treasure-trove of the late Queen's famous wardrobe of 1,000 dresses was raided. Many of Elizabeth's Court ladies still surrounded Anne, and everything contributed to the continuation of the life-style of the past. Queen Anne was no fashion trend-setter. Her portraits, including the one at Hampton Court Palace, painted in 1617 by Van Somer, show her still wearing the Elizabethan French farthingale.

Even after her death in 1617 there was little change until, in 1625, Henrietta Maria, Charles I's French-born wife, burst in upon the stereotyped British fashion scene with a ravishing wardrobe of Parisian elegance reflecting changes that had come to the fore in fashions across the Channel. This produced an immediate revolution in the appearance of British women. The charm and gaiety and *panache* of the Stuarts laid its hold on fashion from this time onwards.

The farthingale disappeared and skirts became flowing and billowy, held out not by artificial cages but by extremely elegant and elaborate petticoats. These now came out into view more than ever before, because skirts, lowered to ground length, were by 1630 being tucked up or looped back with pins or ties to reveal petticoats and to turn this item of underwear into a main part of fashionable outerwear – a

25 Silk gown pinned up at sides to show taffeta petticoat, *c.*1650

26 Dress with split sleeves showing full sleeves of shift, *c.*1650

27 Dress with slit skirt, looped up to show petticoat, *c.*1670. Low neck and short sleeves show shift underneath

recurrent ambivalence through most of fashion history. Petticoats were now more and more elaborately embroidered, quilted, frilled and made in colours that blended with dresses.

The rigid figure dissolved into a new, informal look. The stiff brocades, the jewelled and heavily embroidered silks and velvets gave way to lighter silks, many of them from Lyons, where the silk industry was expanding rapidly. Colours, hitherto strong and violently contrasted, were now softer and more delicate.

The seventeenth century, with its chequered political history, presented a number of fashion swings in a comparatively short time for these days. During the eleven years of the Commonwealth, for instance, fashions became plain and severe among the Roundheads, but an underground movement of the recent gay and elegant Royalist fashions was pursued as a symbol of Cavalier attitudes, ready to burgeon again as soon as the Stuart régime was restored. Skirts with looped-up petticoats continued throughout the century. When from about 1670 trained skirts became fashionable at Court, they too were drawn back and up to form a kind of bustle and to reveal the petticoats, now often of floral silks. Petticoat influence was a main feature of fashion.

In the new fashions the smock also came into the open. The ruff disappeared with the rest of Elizabethan stiff-and-starchedness. The lace-edged neckline of the smock was, however, visible above dé-colletages which became increasingly low. Bodices often had slashed sleeves and nearly always elbow-length ones, through and beneath which were shown to the full the long sleeves of the smock, often immensely wide and ending with deep lace or embroidered frills.

What this focus of attention on the petticoat and the smock meant was that feminine underwear had, for the first time, become sexy, and that what has been accepted as one of its main motivations ever since had come into being. There had been no evidence of this in the past. But the seductive and voluptuous style of dress which developed in seventeenth-century fashion was a mirror of the time, akin to the mood of the Restoration comedies which have intrigued and delighted theatre-goers from that age to our own.

28   17th-century stays

In spite of the new appeal of the petticoat and smock, the actual body remained firmly controlled under 'bodys' which during the seventeenth century began to be called stays, a word which within the century displaced the old term. These stays, usually of heavy linen, came high up on the torso and were stiffened by whalebone. They were shorter-waisted, conforming to the natural figure in this respect. As the century progressed, emphasis on a slim waistline increased and with it a beginning of the kind of tight lacing which was to persist for nearly two centuries among the fashionable, with only one or two brief remissions. This became extreme and led to the epithets 'strait-laced' and 'staid' under the Puritan régime of the mid-century, which, instead of condemning it as an unhealthy and harmful fashion, adopted it and commended it on the grounds that it disciplined the body – a theory which had nothing to do with the original purpose of allurement.

Seventeenth-century fashion reached its heyday when Charles II came to the throne, full of ideas from France, where he and his family and supporters had been in exile. Beautiful silks, an abundance of lace, a profusion of ribbons (worn as a flutter of bows all over the clothes of both men and women) and feathers all bedecked fashion. But the general effect remained much looser and easier than for centuries. Though bodices remained stiff, the provocative effect of a casual and nonchalant look was exploited. It had had no place in Elizabethan fashion. The feeling is voiced by the Cavalier poets, notably by Herrick, who wrote his poem *The Poetry of Dress* about 1650:

> *A sweet disorder in the dress*
> *Kindles in clothes a wantonness:*
> *A lawn about the shoulders thrown*
> *Into a fine distraction,*
> *An erring lace which here and there*
> *Enthrals the crimson stomacher*

A cuff neglectful, and thereby
Ribands to flow confusedly,
A winning wave, deserving note,
In the tempestuous petticoat,
A careless shoe-string, in whose tie
I see a wild civility,
Do more bewitch me, than when art
Is too precise in every part.

It is from this time that actual evidence of what clothes were like begins to build up. The Costume Museum at Bath has early seventeenth-century women's waistcoats and other accessories and also a probably unique complete and very beautiful Restoration dress. Sir Peter Lely's portraits show contemporary seventeenth-century clothes in detail and with a feeling for the effect they produced. The Museum of London has a bodice of blue moiré silk of 1650–1660 and the Victoria and Albert Museum another of about 1660 in white satin. Both these are boned – a fashion which provided a substitute for stays. This was, however, short-lived and by about 1670 the boned bodice had again been displaced by separate stays as a means of shaping the body from under-arms to waist.

From about 1670 the stays became longer, going below the waist at front and back with tabbed side-pieces below the waist stiffened with whalebone to shape the figure there by indenting it at the waist and adding curves at the hips. Such stays were laced back or front and had an increasing amount of whalebone inserted into them and stitched closely in place – always, of course, by hand.

From now on surviving bodices, stays, petticoats and various kinds of hoops and panniers provide ample evidence of the extent to which whalebone, already established as a favourite shapemaker, continued to contribute to the stays, petticoats and artificial devices that gave the feminine figure the contours of fashion and built it up into all the eccentricities that elegance prescribed.

Why, it might well be asked, whalebone? There must be good reasons why whalebone should have remained for centuries the chief material used for shaping stays and corsets and giving them the firmness and figure-controlling qualities which were the main function of the garments. So general was its use that to this day 'bones' are the normal description of corset stiffeners, though almost always the 'bones' now consist of spiral steel or plastic. There are even such contradictory descriptions as 'spiral steel bones' and 'plastic bones'.

The story of whalebone in corsetry is told by Norah Waugh in her *Corsets & Crinolines*. One main reason for its choice was that it had an elasticity, springiness and flexibility that were unequalled by anything else until spiral steels and elastic began to be used, well on in the nineteenth century. It also kept the shape given to it by heating and cooling under compression, which was particularly important in the elaborately waisted eighteenth- and nineteenth-century corset. It could, in addition, be split as finely as could be desired for close boning, without losing its efficiency.

Whalebone originally came from the Bay of Biscay, where there was a whaling industry as early as the twelfth century. In the later Middle Ages whalebones were used as stiffening for headdresses, plumes and the long, fantastically pointed shoes worn by fashionable men in the fifteenth century. By the seventeenth century whales were almost extinct in the Bay of Biscay, but the industry moved to Greenland, where the Dutch were the main operators of it. This lasted until nearly the end of the eighteenth century, during which the vogue for hooped skirts, as well as stiff stays, caused whalebone to be in great demand. By the nineteenth century the Arctic Ocean was replacing the exhausted Greenland whaling grounds, and in the period when the crinoline was in fashion, from about 1855 to 1866, the demand for whalebone was greater than ever before and the shortage of supplies at times became acute. It was opportune that, during the nineteenth century, steel began to replace it, even though steel did not become a really satisfactory corset stiffener until stainless steel began to be used commercially on a large scale after Brearly's discovery in Sheffield in 1912 that it was an ideal material for cutlery.

A further step towards a return to artificial shaping as a feature of fashion began towards the end of the seventeenth century. The looping and bunching up of skirts towards the back during the century had been putting emphasis on that part of the figure, and it was logical that this should lead to the wearing of a bustle. This was sometimes, as in Elizabethan days, called a 'bum roll' and consisted of a pad made of cork or stuffed with some kind of cushion filling. It was tied to the waist and boosted out the figure at the back.

Pepys' diary reflects the interest taken in clothes after the Restoration, although it is noticeable that, like many men of his time, he is far more concerned with his own finery than with his wife's. There are, however, frequent references to what she wore. On 18 August 1660 he says: 'Towards Westminster by water. I landed my wife at Whitefriars with £5. to buy her a petticoat, and my father persuaded her to buy a most fine cloth, of 26s a yard, and a rich lace, so that the petticoat will come to £5: but she doing it very innocently, I could not be angry'. Next day he writes: 'Home to dinner, where my wife had on her new petticoat that she bought yesterday, which indeed is a very fine cloth and a fine lace, but that being of a light colour, and the lace all silver, it makes no great show'. This makes it clear that petticoats were visible to a conspicuous extent and could make a 'great show'.

The smock, stays and petticoat still remained the only underclothing worn. Although drawers had become part of feminine apparel in some continental countries, notably Italy, they were not worn in England until the early nineteenth century. There is no mention of them in records of underwear such as that given by Evelyn's daughter in the description of a fashionable lady in her *Voyage to Marryland*: or *The Ladies Dressing Room Unlock'd*, which mentions various styles of petticoats, including short ones, 'short under Petticoats pure fine, some of Japan Stuff, some of Chine', then 'another quilted white and red, with a broad Flanders lace below'.

She also mentions night smocks adorned with Flanders lace and 'three night gowns of rich Indian stuff', but night gown at that time meant an informal dress, worn by day. A similar meaning seems to be given to it by Pepys, who in 1667 wrote of his wife: 'She ran out in her smock into the aviary . . . and thither her woman brought her her nightgown'. Likewise there was the garment of 1683 described as 'a nightgown of striped Satin cloth colour and Buff'.

4

The Big Build-up of Hoops – and their collapse 1680–1780

By the last years of the seventeenth century the bustle created by the bum roll had evolved into a dome-like cage of wood, cane or metal worn under the skirt and therefore bringing in a new cycle of fashion's changes, another line dependent once again upon the artificial 'booster' of the figure. With the eighteenth century, the casual elegance of the Restoration was outmoded, and within a few years the rounded skirt evolved into something quite new, flattened back and front and extended laterally by hoops contrived in various ways. Later called panniers by the Victorians, these hoops were sometimes almost literally baskets, tied on at the waist on each side. From being modest ovals between about 1715 and 1730, they next became vast side panniers, often extending six feet from side to side.

It was the most ostentatious of fashions, the most arrogant because it could be worn only by those moving in infinite space, walking up and down grand staircases, deferred to when entering rooms. It was for the rich alone, but soon a collapsible version was invented, a contraption of metal which could be telescoped. Examples of various versions exist in museums and costume collections, so they can be studied.

How elaborate was the dress of the early eighteenth century is endorsed by a description in *The Manners and Customs of London in the Eighteenth Century,* which says: 'The ladies must have exhibited a wonderful appearance in 1709; behold one equipped with a black silk petticoat, with a red and white calico border, cherry coloured stays trimmed with blue and silver, a red and dove coloured damask gown flowered with large trees; a yellow satin apron trimmed with white Persian (silk), and muslin head clothes with crow-foot edging, double-ruffles with fine edging, a black silk furbelowed scarf, and a spotted hood'.

The trend of fashion to hoops and panniers, which resembled to some extent the Elizabethan farthingales, is also described in 1711 in

29 Early 18th-century embroidered dress with matching petticoat, visible down the front, and small panniers

the words of Sir Roger de Coverley who, while referring to his family pictures, says: 'You see, Sir, my great-great grandmother has on the new-fashioned petticoat except that the modern is gathered at the waist; my grandmother appeared as if she stood in a large drum, whereas the ladies now walk as if they were in a go-cart'.

30   Silk petticoat of first half of 18th century, embroidered in silk and silver thread in satin stitch and couched work

The hooped petticoat which came into fashion about 1710 was to dominate women's dress for most of that century. This contrivance, reminiscent of the farthingale, passed through various forms, but the general effect was to widen the figure to an extravagant degree at the sides. To start with, however, it was bell-shaped and consisted of three or more hoops of wood, metal or cane, suspended on tapes from the waist. This was the form it took until about 1740. Then it was flattened at back and front and sometimes became a pair of panniers extending at each side. These were sometimes part of the petticoat, the hoops being stitched on to the material of that garment. Sometimes the panniers were a separate contraption, covered with material and attached by tapes at each side of the waist. Soon cane was replaced by whalebone, which was more pliable and more easily manoeuvred for some such heady adventure as getting through doors sideways when wearing hoops.

The fashion was repeatedly attacked by caricaturists, who declared that women looked like donkeys carrying baskets. In 1753 there appeared a pamphlet called 'The Enormous Abomination of the Hoop Petticoat as the Fashion now is'. The amount of space taken up by the hoop was often a social problem. The announcement of the first

31 Cream quilted silk petticoat, with built-in panniers, mid-18th century

32 Augusta of Saxe-Gotha, 1736, by Charles Philips, showing panniers and petticoat

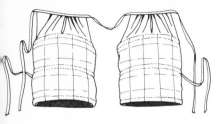

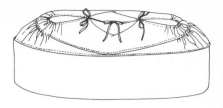

33 Panniers in pink and white checked linen, stiffened with cane, *c*. 1730–50

34 Side hoops of *c*.1750, of cane, covered with green flowered silk

35 Pink Holland hoops stiffened with cane or whalebone, *c*.1770

36 The hoops of 1740, in a dress flattened back and front, with petticoat seen all down the front

37 Robe (1795–1800) with matching petticoat and stomacher of pale blue silk brocaded with coloured silk and silver thread and trimmed with silver lace. Wide panniers

performance of Handel's 'Messiah' in *Faulkner's Journal*, Dublin, 13 April 1742, says: 'The Stewards of the Charitable Musical Society request the favour of the ladies not to come with hoops this day to the Musick Hall in Fishamble Street. The Gentlemen are desired to come without their swords'.

Clothes were still much lighter than in Elizabethan times and as the eighteenth century progressed there was an increasing vogue for dresses of soft, hand-painted silks and for muslins and lawns, giving the floating, negligent look seen in Watteau's paintings. The hooped skirt was not the solid, immovable framework that the farthingale had been. On the contrary, it was always liable to be blown about (and even turned inside out) by the wind or sudden movement or an unwary step. The provocative effect of the exposed ankle or leg was made much of and the plight of the lady whose hooped skirt was swept upwards was the theme of gaily ribald jests among the men of the time. It was also the fashion to give the hooped skirt a slight tilt when walking, so that the under-petticoats became provocatively visible. White stockings, then just coming into fashion, enhanced this effect. In

38   Cotton smock, trimmed with lace, *c.*1747

39   Cotton smock with finely pleated sleeves and low front, *c.*1750

the pseudo-simplicity and elaborate naiveté of the time it was also a favourite diversion of young men to send their young ladies flying gaily through the air on swings. Before this exploit was undertaken the perilous hooped skirt was tied tightly round the wearer's ankles, usually with the man's hat-band, but the possibility of an accident was an intriguing accompaniment of this sport.

By the mid-eighteenth century hoops reached fantastic dimensions. Mrs Delany in her *Life and Letters* said in 1746: 'I don't know what to tell you is in fashion, the only thing that seems general are hoops of enormous size'. Henry Fielding, the novelist, refers to 'seven yards of hoop' and another writer to eight yards. Reproofs about the shortness of the petticoats underneath are also voiced. The petticoats were often no more than calf-length, of light material and very slim. The only other article of underwear worn, apart from the stays, was the chemise, still usually knee-length or longer, so that the raising of the hooped skirt in walking would be very revealing, in terms of what was usually seen of feminine limbs in these days.

About 1760 a new kind of hoop was invented. It consisted of hinged iron hoops worn at each side of the waist. These could be lifted to enable the wearer to pass through narrow spaces. Over this contraption the outer skirt was fitted with immense care, so that among the fashionable scarcely a crease was visible in it.

Unlike the farthingale, which had been more or less limited to Court circles and the wealthy and leisured, the hooped petticoat was widely worn. In its extreme form it did not, however, persist for very long and by about 1780 hoops were going out. After this, false 'rumps' or 'bums' were again being worn, with skirts tucked up or looped back in many folds over full and elaborate petticoats, often quilted in intricate designs or heavily embroidered.

The bodices of dresses worn with these adventurous skirts were, by contrast, tight and rigid. They were usually long-waisted, coming down to a point in front, and under them stiff, heavily boned stays were worn for most of this century. Fashionable men as well as women adopted stays, and girls also wore them continually from a very early age. Examples of these stays still exist and can be examined in costume collections at many museums. Generally speaking, they are made of rather coarse linen or cotton, closely stitched from top to bottom and with row upon row of cane or whalebone inserted in them. Sometimes these stiffeners are so narrow and so near to each other that there is scarcely room for the stitching that separates one from the other. Lacing was usually up the back, with a busk in front, but stays meant for women with heavy figures sometimes had two or three sets of lacing. The fronts of these stays were usually high, the backs even higher, and there were shoulder straps that went either on or off the shoulders, according to the style of dress being worn. Fashionable stays were often brightly coloured and made of very rich materials. One in the collection of historical clothes at Snowshill Manor is in blue damask, others in red silk and green linen.

Sometimes stays were covered with silk or brocade and sometimes with the material of the dress, so that they became the dress bodice. At other times they were embroidered, as were many of those of the following century. They were also at times built into the dress, especially if the latter was a very formal one.

How the corset could be worn as an outer bodice is indicated by an elaborate example dated about 1700, which is in the Victoria and Albert Museum. Made of rose pink watered silk, it is completely boned, as would be expected. The innumerable rows of narrow bones are stitched in so closely as to produce almost the effect of a ribbed material and the garment is completely rigid with them. There is front lacing and the shoulder straps, usual in corsetry until the early nineteenth century, are tied with ribbons at the front. There are two additions to this corset. The first is a long stomacher – a busk-like strip of stiffened material attached under the front lacing. The second is a pair of long, narrow sleeves which are tied on to the straps with ribbons. There is embroidery round the bust, and the bottom of the corset, from the waist, is slashed up a few inches at spaces of two or three inches apart, so that it juts out below the waist. What the sleeves meant is uncertain; it is possible that some kind of sleeveless waistcoat, tunic or overbodice was worn over the corset.

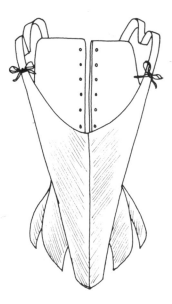

40   Mid-18th-century stays

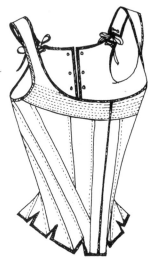

41   Stays of *c*.1775 of maroon figured silk, edged with cream, boned and stitched

A new note of prettiness characterises some other surviving corsets of the late eighteenth century. One, of cream silk, dated about 1780, has front and back lacing, and though it still has straps and points below the waist, it is much softer. Particularly attractive, and of the same decade, is a very different kind of corset. It is made of green glazed cotton with pink silk ribbon edging and pink and white silk embroidered motifs on the boning, which appears only in the front and under the arms. It is, of course, short below the waist, with the usual points, and there are shoulder straps above the straight front which, as usual, pushed up the bust and did not contain it.

Many stays were home-made and instructions for making them began to be published in the ladies' magazines which came into existence at the end of the seventeenth century. These publications became a fruitful source of information on fashion as by the latter part of the eighteenth century many of them carried a fashion article in each issue. At first they were wary of mentioning the 'unmentionable' underclothes, but gradually did so, and in due course, from about the 1870s, underwear advertisements also were included, thus adding to our knowledge of the subject.

Corsetry manufacture had a story of its own, both in Britain and elsewhere. In France Louis XIV formed a company of dressmakers with the right to make many articles of attire, but the staymakers reserved the right to operate exclusively in their own trade. About 1660, also, certain tailors dedicated themselves expressly to staymaking. They were known as *tailleurs de corps* – the last word was still used in French for the corset until well into the eighteenth century.

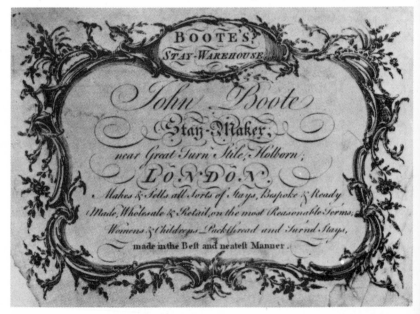

42   A staymaker's trade card, 1766

43 *The Staymaker* by Hogarth

In Britain too the staymaker by the eighteenth century was a special-ist, a highly regarded individual craftsman making bespoke garments for ladies of fashion. Usually he was a man, the most famous in London being Cosins. Many engravings and drawings exist showing ladies of fashion being fitted with their stays, a ritual as complicated as that required for a dress or other outerwear. In a poem of this period called the '*Bassit Table*' and attributed to Lady Mary Wortley Montagu, a description of a young newcomer to town is given in the words of Similinda, an older woman who has befriended her but feels her efforts slighted:

> *She owes to me the very chains she wears –*
> *An awkward thing when first she came to town,*
> *Her shape unfashioned and her face unknown:*
> *I introduced her to the Park and plays,*
> *And by my interest Cosins made her stays.*

For some reason the scene showing the staymaker, a man, fitting a lady with her stays was a favourite subject for illustration by artists. A great number of prints and engravings show this process, sometimes elegantly, but more often with an excess of realism and even as grotesque cartoons, with the lady shown as repulsively ugly and old.

Every town had its staymakers and an unusual record of them in

44   A dress of Spitalfields silk, with quilted petticoat showing under looped-up skirts, *c*.1780. Panniers were by now out of fashion

London and elsewhere is preserved by a substantial number of their trade cards, now in the Department of Prints and Drawings at the British Museum. These are part of a general collection of trade cards made by Mr Ambrose Heal and left by him to the Museum. Many of the cards cannot unfortunately be dated, but an early one, of about 1730, tells that Henry Gough 'maketh women's stays and children's coats after the newest fashion'. (These two items are frequently paired.) Another card, of 1735, belongs to William Mendham who makes 'stays, stomachers, etc, etc'. There is also 'Weatherheads whole-sale stomacher warehouse . . . now selling variety of the newest patterns of busk and millboard stomachers on the most reasonable terms'.

Among eighteenth-century underwear quilted petticoats, worn both for warmth and effect, enjoyed a widespread vogue. One that survives, belonging to about 1730–1740, is in blue satin quilted in a lozenge-shaped design, interlined with cotton-wool and lamb's wool and backed with grey woollen cloth. Others, also still in existence, are in white and pink silk and pale blue and fawn satin, quilted with cotton-wool in elaborate patterns, especially at the hem. Often they are quilted onto a glazed woollen cloth which was known as callamanca.

This elaborate quilting reached its zenith during the latter part of the century but it started about 1740, when skirts were often open in front and looped back to display the quilting. The petticoat was therefore an important part of the dress, but was still called a petticoat. Simple quilting continued for many years for ordinary people. Petticoats during this century were also edged with flounces and frills, and in some cases were made of the same material as the dress. Towards the end of the century another artifice was adopted – a pad that boosted out the bosom, so that the lady projected both before and aft. This was much caricatured at the time, special spoons being suggested in order to make eating a possibility, just as there had been in the days of the ruff.

The nightgown in the eighteenth century could mean a kind of gown worn by ladies, originally as an evening dress. There is thus a reference to 'your brocade nightgown you wore last night' in 1700. From Mrs Delany in 1756 comes a note of 'a nightgown worn without hoops' and in 1778, also in her *Life and Letters*, the observation that 'the Queen was in a hat and an Italian nightgown of purple lutestring'. A 1771 diary notes that the writer called on a bride who was dressed in a white satin nightgown.

45 'Patent Bolsters', Gillray's 1791 caricature of the new fashion for padded bosoms

5

They Threw away their Corsets – but wore bust improvers 1780–1830

From the 1760s to the 1780s fashion seemed to be at one of the most elegant and charming stages of a predictable pattern whereby successive artificial widenings of the figure were followed by less exaggerated styles, both supported by all-important petticoats and based on rigid corsetry. The Elizabethan farthingale had initiated this cycle, the hoops of the earlier eighteenth century had repeated it, as the crinoline was to do less than a century later. A constricted waist and a rigid bodice were accepted as a levy exacted on the wearer by fashion.

The glass of fashion held up by Gainsborough and his contemporary portrait painters towards the end of the eighteenth century presented no shadow of disturbance, but within a decade it had been shattered by a revolution in fashion which in its suddenness and completeness has never had an equal. Accepted types of petticoats, corsets and smocks were discarded along with all known styles of outer dress. High heels, elaborate headdresses, hats and hair styles all disappeared from fashion. So did the wealth of sophisticated accessories and rich jewellery which fashionable women had been sporting for some two hundred years. Instead the vogue was for slim, high-waisted muslin or cotton gowns, clinging to the figure and worn with the minimum of underclothing, sometimes with only flesh-coloured tights beneath them. The *Ladies Monthly Museum* of June 1802 described 'the close, all white shroud-looking, ghostly chemise undress of the ladies, who seem to glide like spectres, with their shrouds wrapt tight about their forms'. In March 1803 it referred to 'young ladies who were dressed or rather undressed in all the nakedness of the mode'.

The French Revolution is often given as the main reason for this extraordinary upheaval in fashion. Class distinctions, it is pointed out, were suppressed and therefore this classless mode of dress was adopted when silks, satins, velvets and all the rest of the accustomed luxury of fashion were abolished, the richer materials actually being banned. In

46   Queen Charlotte, by Sir Thomas Lawrence (1769–1830). Turn-of-the-century elegance with a wealth of gossamer petticoats revealed by looped-back skirts (Reproduced by courtesy of The Trustees, The National Gallery, London)

47   Shift of late 18th or early 19th century with lace and embroidery

48   Fashion changes: gauze dress of 1812–15, worn with long white cotton petticoat

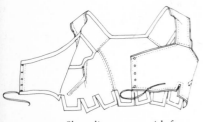

49   Short linen stays with front buttoning, *c.*1790

support of this theory is the fact that the new dress was early adopted by coteries devoted to the new liberal thinking, the chief of them 'Les Merveilleuses', led by Madame Récamier and Madame Tallien. That, however, does not explain the special character of the fashion, so different from anything that had gone before in its pared-down simplicity, its childlike straightness, high waist, tiny sleeves, simple low neck.

It was a fact that little girls, especially English ones, wore this style of dress from the 1780s, before women did. They are seen wearing it in numerous paintings of family groups in which their mothers are still resplendent in panniers and elaborate petticoats. These dresses, and the correspondingly simple skeleton suits of small boys, adopted about the same time, were the first distinctive children's fashions – hitherto children had been dressed as miniature adults. The change was deeply rooted in new, liberal attitudes to children and a new recognition of their distinct needs and rights. Its most obvious motivation was Rousseau's *Emile*, published in 1762 and translated into English in the same year. Although Rousseau had been anticipated to a large degree by earlier educationalists, from Erasmus to John Locke, it was he who made the main impact. He came at the right time; freedom was in the air.

As this freedom built up, it began to affect adult clothes. English fashion was already freer and less formal than that of France, mainly because so much of English life was traditionally centred upon country life. So French fashion started turning to England and the English child's dress, spreading from the small to the not so small girl, was a natural source. The new style, when adopted for women, was known in France as *à l'anglaise*.

The new style of dressing, without any of the accepted complicated underwear, also had affinities with the straight robes seen in Greek statuary and vases, the classical tunics, worn without any supporting or concealing underwear. Devotees of the new French régime rejoiced in harking back to the first famous Republic, that of ancient Greece, which they regarded as the very birth-place of the freedom that Revolutionary France was proclaiming. At the time excavations were rousing new interest in ancient Greece, and it was still thought that the statues in their white marble were as the Greeks had created them – it was not yet realised that originally they had been painted, probably in strong and elaborate colours.

Extreme devotees of the new fashion discarded the corset completely, or reduced it to a narrow band very like the Greek zoné. Others wore very narrow corsets and records of the time tell of a slump in the previously flourishing staymakers' trade. That nothing was worn under the dress seems to be largely mythical, as is the uncorroborated story that dresses were damped to make them cling to the bare body, but underwear was often reduced to a mere single narrow petticoat, sometimes coloured, under the white dress. Another device, calculated to make the style of dress more suited to northern climates, was to add a knee-length overdress, thereby turning a dress into something like an undergarment.

There are frequent references to tights being worn, and they would contribute a certain warmth, if not modesty as then understood. There is a reference in the memoirs of this time which Susan Sibbald wrote in her old age to a curious variation of tights. She describes how, when she was about 18, in 1801–1802, and wearing the new-style muslin dresses as her first grown-up fashions, she also wore an odd kind of tights under her dress. 'The most uncomfortable style of dress', she says, 'was when they were made so scanty that it was difficult to walk in them, and to make them tighter still, invisible petticoats were worn. They were wove in the stocking loom, and were like straight waistcoats . . . but only drawn down over the legs instead of over the arms, so that when walking, you were forced to take short and mincing steps. I was not long in discarding them'.

For those who believe that one constant feature of fashion is to stress one part or another of the female body in order to attract man's interest, the characteristic dress of the Regency and Empire provides a startling example. With the slim sheath arrived the first 'bust improvers'. They were a sufficiently important feature of fashion to spur

50   Full-length white cotton chemise with buttoned tab front, *c.*1800

51   A contemporary engraving satirises the fashion for false bosoms, *c.*1800

52   How it began: a small girl's 'trowsers' seen in a portrait of Lady Mary Howard by John Jackson

53   Cotton open drawers, tucked and trimmed with lace, 1825–30

The Times to say in 1799: 'The fashion for *false bosoms* has at least this utility, that it compels our fashionable fair to wear something'. There are descriptions of these items in various contemporary records. One calls them 'bosom friends', another 'waxen bosoms'. They were made of wax or of stuffed cotton and are shown in illustrations. They disappeared, however, with the change of fashion which began about 1820, and did not reappear until well into Victorian days.

The greatest change in feminine underwear to date from this time was the introduction of drawers. Until the late eighteenth century underwear consisted only of smocks or shifts (the name was changed to chemise about this time, the other terms thenceforth being regarded as vulgar), stays (soon to be described also as corsets) and the highly important petticoats of all kinds. The muslins and lawns used for dresses were not transparent in today's almost literal sense, but they were light and fly-away and with the decimation or discarding of petticoats came the first of many raids on the masculine wardrobe. It began when little girls in the new-style dresses wore under them what were at first called 'trowsers'. These were seen hanging below the dresses, and when women followed suit, their drawers too were visible from about 1790 till 1820. They then disappeared from sight, but those of young girls continued to be seen until well into the second half of the nineteenth century.

There is a hint of earlier appearances of this garment. French and Italian ladies are believed to have worn drawers in the seventeenth century, especially when riding horseback. Catherine de Medici is credited with introducing them to France on marrying Henry II. Pepys mentions his wife's drawers – but she was a Frenchwoman. There is a tantalising statement by Lady Mary Wortley Montagu in 1717: 'The first part of my dress is a pair of drawers, very full, that reach to my shoes', explained perhaps by the fact that she lived for a time in Turkey, where her husband was ambassador.

In England fashion journals made occasional references to drawers from about 1805. That they were accepted in the highest circles by 1811 is testified by royalty itself. The fifteen-year-old Princess Charlotte is on record as 'sitting with her legs stretched out after dinner and shewed her drawers, which it seems she and most young women now wear. Lady de Clifford, the source of this statement, said: "My dear Princess Charlotte, you shew your drawers". "I never do but when I can put myself at ease" ... "Your drawers are much too long". "I do not think so; the Duchess of Bedford's are much longer, and they are bordered with Brussels lace" '. They were therefore acceptable in Lady de Clifford's view. Drawers worn about 1825 by the Duchess of Kent, mother of Queen Victoria, are an exhibit at the Platt Hall Gallery of English Costume. They reach to below the knee, as was usual then, but by 1820 they were invisible and had become literally underwear for women.

'Pantaloons' was at times used to describe 'trowsers' as a type of women's drawers intended to be seen. But the word was also used of masculine leg coverings, and was soon replaced in feminine usage by 'pantalets' or pantalettes. Neither word had much of a vogue for women, and by about 1820 it had been superseded by the persistent 'drawers'.

The claim that women had discarded their corsets towards the end of the eighteenth century had about as much – or as little – truth as the boast that they had burned their bras in the 1960s. A few of the young, for a few years, probably ceased to wear corsets, but short ones were frequently worn. For those whose figures needed some flattery a long corset, reaching down to the hips, instead of ending with tabs just below the waist, was a notable feature of underwear from about 1800 to 1811.

Introduced at the same time were corsets which had cup-shaped bust sections inserted into them instead of merely pushing up the bosom or flattening it, as had previously happened. Then, as the Regency style went out of date, curves were aided by the addition of below-waist gussets in corsets. In 1816 a further extension of this trend came in the oddly named Divorce Corset which did not refer to marital disagreement but to the separation of one breast from the other by means of a padded triangle of iron or steel which was inserted into the centre front of the corset with its point upwards. It was similar to the principle of the modern brassière, but it was short-lived and left no impression on the solid Victorian shelf-like bust.

There was a depression in the staymaking business when, from about 1800 to 1830, women of fashion took to clinging 'classical' gowns and gave up wearing corsets. But after 1830 fashion reverted to its more elaborate tradition and the staymakers came back into prominence. By this time considerable numbers of women were following this trade, among them being Mrs Bevern, 'Patent Stay and Corset Maker', of 50 Burlington Street, London. Her trade card shows a picture of a young lady in the still slim, high-waisted dress of the early 1800s. S. Gardner, 'French Stay & Corset Maker' of Long Acre, 'where ladies may be fitted with good stays (ready made) from 15s to 23s', explains on the trade card that Mrs G. is 'daughter to Mr Meggitt, Staymaker, Holborn'.

By the 1830s the staymaker was expanding his (or her) business and either had a workroom or employed ten or twelve outworkers. Entry to the craft was by apprenticeship. The staymaker, however, as an independent craftsman did not survive the arrival of the sewing machine and the mechanisation of corset manufacture in factories. He

54 A ball dress of 1829 shows how far fashion has moved from its recent simplicity, and how much more underwear is needed

either became absorbed in the new régime or went out of business.

A practical development in corsetry was the patent taken out by Rogers of London in 1823 for metal eyelets for corset lacings, but the modern style of eyelet was devised by Daude of Paris and came into use in 1828.

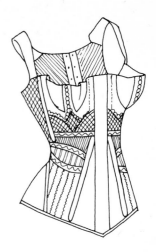

55 Young girl's petticoat with attached top, in white corded cotton, *c*.1830

56 Linen chemise of 1835

57 Stays with gussets, of cotton, boned and stitched, 1830

In 1839 Jean Werly, a Frenchman, made a landmark in corset history when he took out a patent for woven corsets made on a loom. They were popular until about 1890 and were significant as the first step towards the machine-made corset.

Although so much less underwear was worn from the end of the eighteenth century, in some ways it became more important. The idea of physical cleanliness had not been given much importance in the past, but it was pursued with extreme zeal by the Macaronis, those famous dandies of the 1770s, and was raised to being almost the ultimate test of good breeding and gentility by Beau Brummell. It pervaded society steadily, becoming part of fashion and leading to underwear being given more attention, being changed more frequently and therefore possessed in larger quantities. From this time on it attracted much more attention and acquired increasing variety.

Rue de la Paix, 13, et rue du Ponceau, 2, carré Saint-Martin.

CORSETS EN TOUS GENRES.

Corsets Josselin, à mécaniques et à délaçages. Ces corsets, qui habillent dans la perfection, amincissent et allongent la taille sans la comprimer; on les lace, délace, serre et desserre en une seconde, sans aucun dérangement pour la toilette. Ils ont valu à M. Josselin, breveté, seul inventeur, quatre rapports et trois médailles de l'Académie royale de médecine, de plusieurs Sociétés savantes et des Expositions de 1834 et 1839. Il est aussi inventeur des agrafes hygiéniques pour robes, et des boucles à cylindre pour ceintures de robes.

58 Paris corset advertisement of 1840, showing gussets

6

A Time of Change: Drawers and Bloomers 1830–1856

By about 1820 the pared-down, figure-clinging style of dress had disappeared and a start had been made on the build-up of outer garments and, even more, on the growth in the number and variety of undergarments which was to be a dominant feature of fashion for the rest of the century. Victorian materialism and the rise of the great, increasingly numerous and prosperous middle classes, socially ambitious and class-conscious, were part of an immense social revolution of which fashion would carry the imprint in its own ways. More and more of the populace were going to be involved in fashion as clothes manufacture and retailing grew and developed.

After the long, straight corset of 1800–1811, which was suited to a more or less straight fashion line, there came a shorter but stiffer version which pushed up the bust but was mainly designed to emphasise the waist and, very soon, to pull it in with the utmost severity of tight lacing, which was to continue for the rest of the century and even beyond it. Doctors were to condemn it, writers and others to decry and deplore it, cartoonists to satirise it, but it continued to be a main essential of the fashionable look. It was encouraged by fashionable schools. Mothers regarded it as necessary to their young daughters' future social success. There is one horrifying account, ascribed to as early a date as 1810, asserting that it was not unusual to see 'a mother lay her daughter down upon the carpet, and, placing her foot on her back, break half a dozen laces in tightening her stays'. There were claims galore that, if started early, tight lacing would not be painful or damaging to the health. Despite the arguments and protests it went on. There were, however, a few palliatives, including light-weight corsets for what we would call casual wear, during the day in the house. There was also the introduction of the peignoir or negligée – something between a dressing gown and outerwear, which could be worn without a corset and which became famous from the 1870s to the end of

Progress of the Toilet — THE STAYS. *Plate 1*

Edwardian days as the tea gown, another example of underwear becoming outerwear.

The chemise remained unchanged in shape at this period, still around knee-length, wide and sometimes with sleeves. Drawers became more generally worn, extending to almost all the middle classes and becoming a status symbol of all but the poorest. The main feature of women's underwear was, however, once again the petticoat – or rather petticoats, because the multiplication of this garment was an outstanding feature of underwear of the first half of the nineteenth century. The fashionable outline was, year by year, becoming more closely waisted, more full in the skirts, and under these skirts went not one but several petticoats, under ones of flannel or plain cotton, with

the final one probably embroidered or lace-trimmed, but at this time
puritanically white.

From the 1820s there was a return of the bustle, first as a small,
down-stuffed or cotton-stuffed pad at the back, but before 1840 as a
larger and more extensive addition to the natural figure, reaching
round to the sides, sometimes fortified with whalebone. It was tied on
at the waist, not attached to the petticoat. It was worn by all classes.
Jane Welsh Carlyle in a letter of 1834 wrote: 'The diameter of fashionable ladies at present is about three yards, their bustles (false bottoms)
are the size of an ordinary sheep's fleece. The very servant girls wear
bustles; Eliza told me of a maid of theirs went out on Sunday with
three kitchen dusters pinned on as a substitute'.

In the 1840s, there was a still further widening of the skirts by means
of a combined bustle-petticoat of horsehair fabric – called 'crinoline'

61   A corset of 1831

from the French word *crin*, meaning horsehair, which in turn came from the Latin *crinis*, plus the French *lin* or Latin *linum*, thread. It was to be confusing to future fashion students that the same word was used for the cage framework of the 1850s and 1860s.

In 1851 fashion for the first time had a spanner thrown into its works – the start of a series to be directed against the established order which had persisted for about 300 years, only briefly disturbed by the turn of the century upheaval. Mrs Amelia Bloomer launched in America the famous outfit which was known by her name and which had a considerable vogue there, being linked with the rising agitation for women's rights. She was not, however, its inventor but was a journalist and author promoting, in the interests of rational dress for women, an outfit created by Elizabeth Smith Miller, who wore it on a visit to Seneca Falls, NY, where Amelia Bloomer lived and where she

62 *(left)* Mrs Amelia Bloomer, a woodcut published by her in *The Lily,* the magazine which she edited from 1849 to 1858. She considered it a good picture of the dress which was given her name

63 *(right)* The Bloomer outfit as worn in 1895

saw and admired it. Aimed at freeing women from the discomforts and folly of conventional fashion, it was not very alarming by today's standards, but in Britain at that time it was regarded variously as horrifying, immodest, ridiculous, hideous. Men reviled it as an attempt by women to 'wear the trousers'. In *Punch* and on the stage it had a brief furore. What in fact it consisted of was a simple bodice approximating fairly closely to what was in vogue, with a slightly flaring skirt which reached well below the knees, but under this were seen baggy, Turkish-style trousers reaching to the ankle, usually edged with a lace frill. Its sponsors believed that the Bloomer fashion was feminine and attractive as well as sensible.

A very few doughty spirits wore it in Britain, but it made next to no impact on fashion at the time. Fifty years later it came into its own, when women began riding bicycles and for this they wore bloomers. Soon after that bloomers became the name of a style of feminine drawers or knickers which had a great vogue in the early twentieth century, especially under sports clothes and schoolgirls' gym tunics.

For its failure at the time of its appearance Mrs Merrifield, whose *Dress as a Fine Art* (1854) is one of the most enlightening and enlightened books on fashion at this time, says: 'We are content to adopt the greatest absurdities in dress when they are brought from Paris or recommended by a French name, but American fashion has no chance of success in aristocratic England'.

In the year of the Bloomers' rallying-call to dress reform, corsets were a considerable feature of the section of the Great Exhibition of 1851 devoted to 'Articles of clothing for immediate personal or domestic use'. Surprisingly, many of the thirty-odd designers and manufacturers who displayed corsets claimed that the garments had features aimed at comfort and convenience, for it was a time when fashion seemed to be as awkward and uncomfortable as it had ever been. But Caroline Joubert, inventor and manufacturer, of Maddox Street, Hanover Square, showed a 'self-adjusting white watered corset, with a spring busk and improved lacing'. George Roberts, of Oxford Street, a manufacturer, had a corset made in 21 pieces, all cut on the cross upon the expanding principle, with instant relieving backs. Charlotte Smith of Bedford, described as an inventress, showed 'Patent symmetrical corsets, enabling the wearer to regulate the pressure of the stays (as may be required) in a simple manner'. There was emphasis on seamless corsets and many corsets were woven (therefore among the first to be machine-made). Corsets made 'to fasten and unfasten instantaneously without lacing' were also included and elastic ones which allowed for freedom in breathing were much favoured.

Unfortunately the panel of judges which made awards did not think much of British corset designers or makers and the top prizes went to French and Belgian exhibitors. They found 'but few specimens in which there is novelty combined with useful improvement', but while denying that any great advances had been made in the past five years they found that 'there can now be obtained by all classes, a well-formed and good corset at a very moderate price', which was desirable for 'an article of such universal and fashionable use'.

The only British prize medallist in corsetry was Madame Roxy Caplin, for 'Corsets, ingeniously adapted for giving support to the trunk without confinement of the thorax', which, improbably, she exhibited in the section devoted to Philosophical, Musical, Horological and Surgical instruments, away from all the other corset exhibits. She listed her entries as 'the Hygeianic corsets. The registered corporiform corsets, plain and mechanical. The new contracting back Abdominal suspenders. . . . The child's bodice, also the reversotractor to prevent children standing on one leg, with a variety of other Hygeianic adaptations made in accordance with the science of anatomy and physiology'. She was to write a book *Health and Beauty or Woman and her Clothes* about ten years later, urging the importance of corsets in promoting or ruining health, and she wrote and lectured on health and physiology. Dr Elizabeth Blackwell, the first woman to qualify as a doctor, praised her as 'the first who has made the corset tolerable in the eyes of a physician'. The wife of a doctor and a student of the medical side of corsetry, Madam Caplin gave the idea of health corsets its first large-scale publicity and its first success.

It was, however, from America that there came to England, four years after Amelia Bloomer and the Great Exhibition, the sewing machine, an invention which was to transform the whole concept of outerwear and underwear and to affect the latter sooner and more basically. From the earliest attempts to create a machine that would take over the appallingly tedious labour of sewing garments by hand, corsets were seen as a prime outlet for such an invention.

The idea of a machine to do stitching was first conceived by an Englishman, Thomas Saint. In 1790 he was granted a patent on a machine for sewing leather and his drawings of it show certain features essential to the modern sewing machine. He devised the overhanging arm, the up-and-down movement of the needle, the horizontal bed or plate to support the sewing, and also the use of a continuous thread. He appears, however, never to have put his innovation to practical use.

The first man to obtain a patent and exercise his right to it was a poor French tailor, Barthelemy Thimmonier. By 1829 he had produced a sewing machine which made a chain stitch by means of a hooked needle like a crochet hook. In 1830 he took out his patent, and by 1831 eighty of his machines were making uniforms for the French army.

These machines were, however, destroyed by a mob, who, like the Luddites in the case of the spinning jenny and other craftsmen throughout industrial history when confronted by new machines, thought their jobs were being threatened by the mechanical contrivance that did their sewing for them.

Thimmonier went back to his home, but he persevered with his invention. By 1845 he had developed it so far that it could sew two hundred stitches a minute and could be used on all kinds of materials from muslin to leather.

He took out patents in England in 1849, and in the USA in 1850, but by this time he had missed the big opportunity. Other inventors were in the field with more practical machines. He died in poverty in 1857 at the age of 64.

From England and France the initiative in sewing machine invention had passed to America, but it took the labours of a generation of inventors there to make the sewing machine a really practical manufacturing device. The first man to produce a sewing machine containing nearly all the essential parts of the best modern machines was an American Quaker, Walter Hunt, who also invented the safety-pin. His was a lock-stitch machine, using an eye-pointed needle which worked in combination with a shuttle carrying a second thread.

In 1838 Hunt suggested to his daughter Caroline that she should start manufacturing corsets on one of his machines, but she was afraid to do so – for the familiar reason that it might put the hand-stitchers out of work and create unrest. Discouraged, Hunt sold out his invention to George Arrowsmith, but it fell into disuse and his machine lay forgotten in a garret for fifteen years.

To Elias Howe must be given credit for setting the sewing machine fair and square on its way to being the accepted means of clothing production of all kinds. He invented a lock-stitch machine and, although he lacked Hunt's original inventive talent, he had persistence and confidence in himself. These were qualities needed for the big drive, now about to start in earnest, to get rid of a centuries-old tradition of slow, laborious hand-sewing and to hand the work over to operators working at sewing machines of ever-increasing speed, versatility and efficiency. Unfortunately, however, Howe did not possess all the organisational qualities needed to go the whole way towards securing all-over acceptance of the elusive machine. In 1847 he came from America to England and, after eight months' hard work, adapted his invention to the requirements of a Mr William Thomas, who manufactured corsets, by hand-labour of course, in his shop in Cheapside. But for some reason this venture did not bring the expected break-through.

Meantime, back in America, several ingenious mechanics who had seen Howe's machine were working on his ideas, involving him in a long series of legal disputes and difficulties.

The break-through to success was achieved by Isaac Merrit Singer, the first man to produce a practical sewing machine and to bring it into general use, first in America and then in England.

In 1851 Singer developed the idea of the reciprocating shuttle. In addition, he introduced a positive mechanical feed, and the needle bar which had pushed horizontally was replaced by a straight needle which worked up and down. This was the first lock-stitch machine to do continuous stitching, the lack of which was the biggest defect in the Howe machine. Singer also invented the yielding vertical presser foot to hold the work in place. He first took out a patent for his machine on 12 August 1851, and in that year the firm of I.M. Singer & Co was established.

The experience of Walter Hunt with the corset trade as an outstanding sphere of usefulness for the sewing machine was repeated by Singer, but this time with happier results. The first sewing machines to be brought into Britain were seen in America in 1855 by Mr Robert Symington, a young member of the Market Harborough family which had already laid the small foundations of what was to become an immense corset company. Robert Symington did not make the fortune he had hoped for in his impetuous venture to the New World at the age of eighteen, but he brought back something which led the way to fortune at home and was probably in the long run much more valuable. He brought three of the new sewing machines and had them installed in the Market Harborough cottage workroom where corset-making was presided over by his mother.

While Singer was trying out his sewing machine, a similar line of experiment, quite unrelated to his, was proceeding in Adrian, Michigan. Here early in 1849 Allen Benjamin Wilson, who had never seen or even heard of the Howe machine, invented a sewing machine.

A Mr Wheeler saw Wilson's invention in New York, went into partnership with Wilson, and superintended the manufacture of the new machines. Wilson invented the rotary hook and a patent was taken out for this on 12 August 1851 – the same day that Isaac Singer was granted the patent for his first machine. Wilson also patented the first stationary circular disc bobbin, which was a basic innovation in sewing machine construction. Of all the sewing machine pioneers, Wilson was the most original and many of his devices are still embodied in the machines of today.

The last of the sewing machine pioneers was James Gibbs, from Virginia. His curiosity about machine stitching was roused by seeing a picture in a paper, and then by watching an early Singer machine working in a tailor's shop in 1850. In his view the machine was far too

64 *(left)*   Wheeler and Wilson sewing machine of the late 1880s

65 *(right)*   Singer sewing machine of the late 1890s, used especially for the manufacture of corsets and other women's wear. It was fitted with from three to twelve needles, and could carry out parallel rows of fine lock-stitching

clumsy, complicated and expensive, and he set to work to produce something simpler, cheaper and more practical. His chief original invention was the chain stitch machine, very much as we know it today. Gibbs showed his work to James Wilcox, who was so impressed that he suggested a working partnership. The Wilcox and Gibbs sewing machine, which was the means of developing Gibbs' ideas, was to play an important part in the subsequent development of the machine.

It is, incidentally, a curious fact that when it was shown at the Great Exhibition of 1851 the sewing machine attracted very little attention. It was not even mentioned in reviews of the Exhibition. None the less the sewing machine from this time onwards came increasingly into use and it was to be largely responsible for an entirely new conception of clothing, a new era of mass production, an increasing rapidity in fashion changes and, not least, the development of corsetry and underwear manufacture as a major industry with a turnover of many millions of pounds a year.

7

Dressed to Kill, with crinolines and tight lacing 1856–1865

By about 1856 the weight and bulk of petticoats exceeded anything seen in the past and made a remarkable contrast to the ethereal underwear of half a century before. The appearance of the fashionable lady of the time is detailed in *Modes and Manners* by Fischel and Von Boeke: 'In 1856 the underclothing of a lady of fashion consisted of long drawers trimmed with lace, a flannel petticoat, an under-petticoat three and one half yards wide, a petticoat wadded to the knees, and stiffened on the upper part with whalebones inserted a handsbreadth from one another, a white starched petticoat with three stiffly starched flounces, two muslin petticoats, and finally the dress'. There would also, presumably, be a chemise and a severe corset under all that.

The crinoline or, to distinguish it from the previous horsehair petticoat, the 'cage' crinoline, came into the fashion picture at this point, and though it was to be ridiculed and denounced even more than earlier excesses of fashion, it was a liberation to limbs previously pent beneath so many petticoats. According to one writer it was, briefly, 'a light metal or whalebone structure in which hoops were placed horizontally one above the other and held together by curved ribs'. Alternatively, tapes held the tiers of hoops in place. The petticoats, except for one slim one, could be discarded. Charles Gibbs-Smith in *The Fashionable Lady in the Nineteenth Century* states more specifically that 'the "Artificial crinoline" consists of concentric whalebone, wire or watch-spring hoops suspended on strips of material, with or without covering fabric'.

Just how, when and where it originated is also in some doubt. The English couturier Charles Frederick Worth, who dominated the Paris fashion world at the time, is generally credited with having introduced it. One of his biographers, Edith Saunders, says: 'Conflicting tales have been told about the origin of the cage, but Madame Carette, one of the Empress Eugénie's Ladies-in-waiting, says that it was introduced by

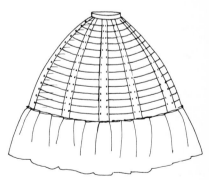

66 Crinoline of *c.*1858 made of vertical bands of tape with rows of steel and pleated frill

67 Promenade dresses of about 1840, with many petticoats (from *Petit Courrier des Dames*)

Worth, and Jean Philippe (son of J.F.) says the same thing. An English inventor, according to his account, brought the crinoline to his father, who saw its possibilities at once and proceeded to launch it. On the other hand, those still living who have heard Worth talk of it in their youth are certain he detested the crinoline, and there is no doubt that, when it was firmly established, he was its most energetic opponent and was responsible at last for its overthrow. But it seems likely that on first seeing it he was momentarily carried away by enthusiasm'.

The exact date of the introduction of the crinoline has also been the subject of dispute and research. In her life of Queen Victoria, Lady Longford confirms and adds to the link with the Empress Eugénie and gives a precise date: April 1855, when the Emperor and Empress visited the Queen and Prince Albert at Windsor: 'The Queen', says Lady Longford, 'was charmed to learn that Prince Albert admired Eugénie's *toilette* excessively. She had in fact brought the first crinoline to England – grey with black lace and pink bows, and a wreath of pink chrysanthemums in her auburn hair'.

Alison Gernsheim in *Fashion and Reality 1840–1914*, an admirably researched study based on the matchless Gernsheim collection of photographs of the fashions of the period, delves further into all origins of the crinoline, from English and German sources. She finds that as early as 1853 some dressmakers were on record as inserting whalebone hoops into skirt linings, that in the following year *The Ladies Companion* suggested 'putting pieces of straw underneath each flounce to stiffen it, with the comment: "The hoops of our grandmothers cannot have been much wider than the skirts of the fashionable lady of the present day"'. There were also various records about this time of inflatable rubber tubes being used to form a bell-like framework for one version of the crinoline. One patent noted by Alison Gernsheim

68 Another version of the crinoline, showing petticoat and drawers, *c.*1856

was taken out in May 1856 for a garment inflated by means of bellows and deflated to enable the wearer to sit down: 'presumably she had to carry the bellows about in order to re-inflate when she stood up again'.

At the same time numerous stiff, starched, frilled muslin petticoats were still being worn to create the same effect by less drastic means.

The metal crinoline, which was to dominate fashion for more than ten years from 1856, had the great merit of lightness, and most fashionable women welcomed it rapturously for this and for the freedom of having their limbs (legs was still a coarse word) unencumbered by heavy layers of petticoats. Mrs Gernsheim, alone among fashion writers, tracks down its inventor as R.C. Millet of Besançon, whose British agent, C. Amet, 'was granted the first British patent for a metal crinoline in July 1856 – "skeleton petticoat made of steel springs fastened to tape"'. This, she adds, was British patent No. 1729, 22 July 1856. The specification of 'tape' left loopholes for other firms to create a highly competitive market by manufacturing a variety of crinolines. The biggest of them was the corset firm of Thomson, who employed 1,000 women in their London factory and produced 4,000 crinolines a day. They also had a vast output in a factory in Saxony. The link between the crinoline and the Empress Eugénie is supported by the fact that one 1856 style of crinoline was called the Parisian Eugénie Jupon Skeleton Petticoat. An immense number of designs was evolved, mostly using steel watch-spring, with the wheels ranging from nine to eighteen in number according to the formality of the dress. The *Sansflectum* of 1861 had hoops covered with gutta-percha and was washable. There were devices to make sitting down easy, and even hinges to facilitate entry through doorways and the ascent of stairs.

In magazines of the early 1860s there are advertisements for Sansflectum crinolines: 'The latest novelty which the Ladies have to be thankful for is the Patent Sansflectum skirt. 21s. 25s. 28s. and 33s, others 15/6, 18/6, 21s.'. Muslin covers are offered at 3/6, Alpaca at 5/11. The Ondina or Wave Jupon costs 15/6, 18/6, or 21/–. It did not cost much to follow fashion.

The crinoline grew continuously larger in the years after 1856. The space it took up made social life complicated and provided endless scope for quips and cartoons in *Punch*. It was so difficult for women to get on to buses wearing it that there was a suggestion (pictured in a *Punch* cartoon) that crinolines should be shed and hung up outside the vehicle. As the cage was also light and volatile, there were endless accidents. The Duchess of Manchester tripped on a stile during a country walk and is recorded by Lady Stanley as falling head over heels in full view of the attendant company; luckily she was at least wearing red tartan drawers underneath.

Various devices were invented to make the crinoline less unmanage-

69   The problem of boarding a bus in a crinoline (from *Punch*, 22 December 1860)

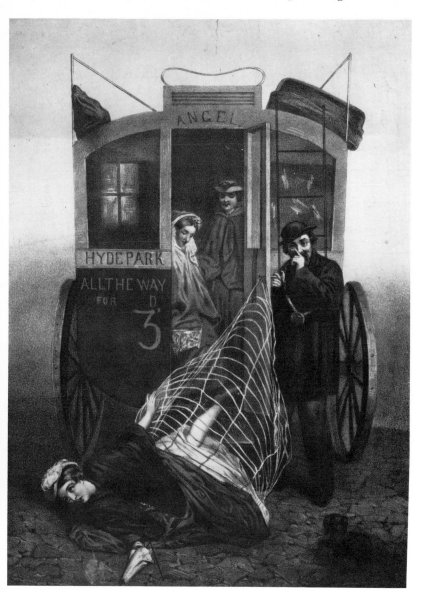

able; of these the Pompadour consisted of a series of strings, apparently pulled like a Venetian blind, 'the length and width of dresses rendering it quite indispensable to hold them up, a new mode of doing this will, we think, be welcome to our readers'. So ran the advertisement. Why not shorten or slim down the skirts, one might ask.

Arnold Bennett in his *Old Wives Tale* recounts a similar episode in less exalted life, when the two young girls, Sophia and Constance, un-pack their mother's newly delivered crinoline and Sophie tries it on. 'Her mother's tremendous new gown ballooned about her in all its fantastic richness and expensiveness.' But disaster soon followed:

'Then Sophia fell, in stepping backwards; the pyramid was over-balanced, great distended rings of silk trembled and swayed gigantically on the floor and Sophia's small feet lay like the feet of a doll on the rim of the largest circle, which curved and arched above them like a cavern's mouth. . . . The girls regained their feet, Sophia with Constance's help. It was not easy to right a capsized crinoline'. In this case the skirt seems to have been attached to or at least delivered with the under-cage.

Apart from its social inconveniences, the crinoline had other more serious drawbacks. Unlike the farthingale and hoops, it was worn by all classes in the new manufacturing age, when it could be machine-made and when the accompanying wide skirts and fitted bodices could be produced by the recently invented sewing machine.

The crinoline was worn therefore by women factory workers and caused havoc where china, glass and other delicate materials were being made, as finished objects were swept off shelves by passing cages. A German visitor of 1865 noted peasant girls working in fields in crinolines. In strong winds wearers could be blown off their feet. One trembles for the crinolined lady seen in a photograph of climbers on the Grindelwald glacier about 1863; she had evidently just climbed up a long, steep ladder and was perched on a narrow, precarious ledge. More serious was the danger from fire. It was only too easy for the extended skirt to sweep right up to an open grate, and the wire frame-work made it impossible to wrap the victim in the recommended rug to extinguish the flames. Evening dress fabrics included highly in-flammable tulle, net and muslin and the crinoline brought death or disfigurement to many wearers as a result. Magazine articles of the 1860s gave repeated warnings of the frightful risks inherent in the crinoline.

It has been said that Queen Victoria was opposed to the crinoline, but in addition to her repeated and enthusiastic admiration for the dress of the Empress Eugénie, its most famous exponent, there are many photographs showing crinolines worn in Court circles: by the Queen herself in a charming photograph with Prince Albert in 1861; by her eldest daughter, the Princess Royal (a particularly beautiful evening version with deep tiers of lace) in 1859; by groups at Osborne and at country houses; also by Princess Alice and the elegant Princess of Wales, later Queen Alexandra, at Sandringham in 1863.

Bodices throughout the crinoline decade remained tightly fitting and often boned. Boned corsets, high on top and supporting the bust with the aid of gussets, were worn and they also had gussets below the waist. Tight lacing persisted, but it was less extreme during the crinoline era than before or after, mainly because the great width of the skirts made the waist look narrower, an effect also enhanced by the very wide

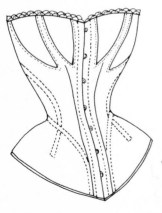

71 Front-fastening corset with patent clips, *c.*1862

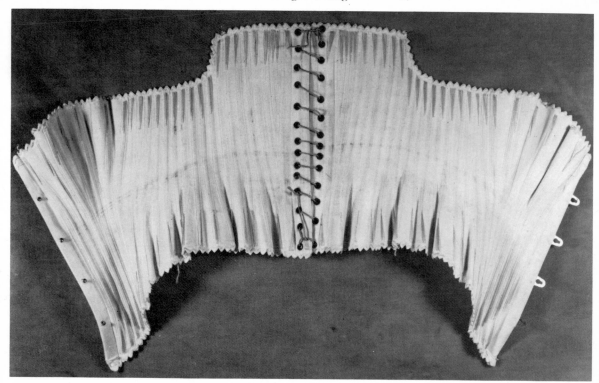

sleeves, often lavishly frilled from shoulder to elbow, which were fashionable.

The old idea of under-sleeves, part-lingerie, was also revived and they appeared below the heavy, frilled shorter sleeves. They were often part of a bodice or camisole, a new addition to underwear from about the middle of the century, which had the prime purpose of protecting the corset. The Garibaldi shirt, introduced as a fashion on the wave of enthusiasm for that hero's invasion of Sicily in 1860, included various blouse-like designs, worn by women under dress bodices and showing the sleeves, as underwear had done in the past. Chemises and drawers continued to be made as previously, but were somewhat more decorative and at times made of finer longcloth. Nightdresses were still white, wide and bulky, but with the development of machine-made underwear at moderate prices they were bought in larger quantities. The vast Victorian trousseau, with a dozen of every item of underwear as the general rule, came into being among the middle classes.

Petticoats again came into prominence in the 1860s, when the crinoline was at times drawn up for walking, revealing quite a lot of the petticoat beneath it. A special type of crinoline which could be hitched up in this way was called the *cage américaine*. The Empress Eugénie described how she wore a short crinoline, only slightly below the knees, for country wear. There was also a continued vogue for frilly

72 A corset of *c.*1860, worn for riding

73 Boned corset in blue silk, *c.*1864

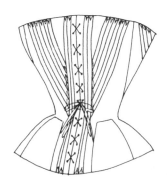

muslin petticoats, for lace-trimmed ones and also for warm flannel ones, for there were some women who preferred these to the cage crinoline. Florence Nightingale determinedly refused to wear the cage style. So did Jane Welsh Carlyle, though she was a close follower of fashion.

Another underwear change which started in the 1860s was the introduction of coloured petticoats. This was a fashion triggered off by the discovery of aniline dyes, the first of which, a bright purple, was produced by William Henry Perkin (later Sir William) in 1858, to be followed by others, chief favourites of fashion being magenta and solferino, both named after the victories of Napoleon III over the Austrians in 1859. Coloured petticoats were to be fashionable in great variety and at moderate prices from that time onwards. From the mid-nineteenth century the corset had continued to change in shape and construction to a considerable extent, just as did the outer fashions to which it lent much of their form. Up to the 1840s corsets still had shoulder straps and at that time they also had pronounced rounded cup-shaped bust sections. Gussets were also inserted to shape hips and busts.

The shaping of corsets by joining up separate pieces instead of by adding gussets to one-piece garments began in the late 1840s and became very popular in the 1850s. Cording and quilting were also in vogue, and the corset was sometimes worn over the crinoline and petticoats, so as to achieve the smallest possible waist. In colour white was the most elegant choice, but grey, putty, red and black were also used for practical reasons.

Corsets still came high above the waist and throughout the crinoline era – from the 1850s to the late 1860s – they still contained the bosom. The stiff front busk was a continuing feature and it lasted during the time when the front fastening, introduced in the early 1830s, gradually ousted complete dependence upon back lacing as the only way of putting on or taking off the corset.

In the late 1860s another contribution was made to the strict shaping of the corset by the introduction of steam-moulding. This meant that the corset, when stitched together and made up, with its busk and bones, was heavily starched and dried and stiffened by being placed on a steam mould made in the desired shape. It therefore became 'set' in its shape. One of these moulds still exists at Symington's corset collection at Market Harborough. It is a hollow copper shape, fixed to a bench, and the steam was 'fed' into it from a series of pipes running under the bench and up into the mould.

74 Underwear of 1860–65: wool hose made by Corah and crinoline supported by red flannel

8

Showing the Figure – but with bustles behind 1865–1880

The crinoline had brought some small relaxation of the extremities to which tight lacing had been carried as well as eliminating the bulk and weight of petticoats. It began to diminish in the early 1860s, the first sign of change being a flattening of the front and a backward movement of the wide circle of its framework. By this time the whole structure had lost its social prestige and was being mass-produced for all at low prices. In an increasingly class-conscious age it was due to be replaced with something which the top people could at least enjoy credit for being the first to introduce.

The crinoline disappeared somewhat suddenly about 1865. There is on record a story that its chief protagonist, the Empress Eugénie, created a stir when she suddenly appeared in a flat-front dress unsupported by the cage. This was soon followed with Worth, at the height of his fashion reign, campaigning strenuously for the abolition of something which had become stale and was inhibiting the change which is the essence of fashion. By the late 1860s crinolines were out so far as fashion was concerned.

The new line of fashion followed the figure to the extent that it

75   Crinoline with flat front and wide ruched back, 1872

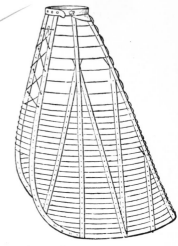

76   Flattened version of Thomson's Safety Crinoline, 1868, showing a further change in the fashion line

77 (*left*)   Corsets of 1875, as seen in an advertisement from *La Mode Illustrée*

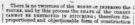

IZOD'S PATENT CORSETS.

STEAM-HEATED LAY FIGURES FOR CORSET MANUFACTURE.

There is no TWISTING of the BONES or INJURING the FIGURE, and by this process the SHAPE of the CORSET CANNOT BE DESTROYED IN STITCHING; therefore disproportioned and objectionable form of construction

78   Corset of *c.*1879 with long curved front-fastening busk

accentuated the bust, defined the waist very closely and then showed every curve of the hips. This gave a new importance to the corset which became increasingly shaped, with close cording as well as boning contributing to its rigidity. The stiff front busk became more pronounced as, from the mid 1860s, the skirt of the dress was drawn tightly over the front of the figure.

The backward sweep of the skirt was often achieved by looping it back, once more revealing the petticoat, or, more exactly, the top petticoat because these garments began multiplying again as the decade neared its close. By the late '60s a very becoming flat-fronted, backward-sweeping skirt was fashionable, worn without the crinoline. Trains developed, and were favoured by the fashionable – George Du Maurier shows young women already wearing them in a *Punch* drawing of 1865. They presented problems out of doors, and the next development was to bunch them up, showing the petticoat again in front. Bunching up was soon not enough, and by the beginning of the 1870s underwear was again being enhanced by various styles of artificial aids, called tournures or, less elegantly, bustles, which remained in fashion for two or three years, disappeared, but recurred in an enlarged form about a decade later. The bustle was often a kind of steel birdcage, covered with material, and by the early 1870s it extended down to the knees, becoming a kind of half-crinoline.

By the mid-1870s the bustle had been superseded by something like

79 *(left)*   Dress of 1873–5, with back drapery and petticoat effect in front

80 *(right)*   Crinoline of 1860s and crinolette of 1870s

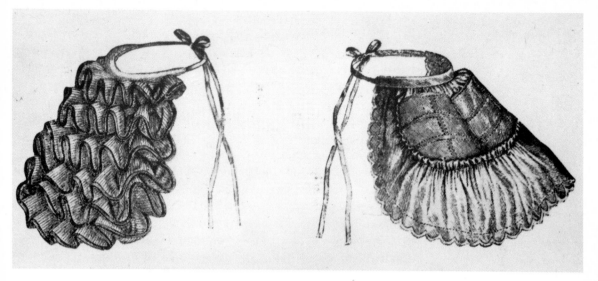

a revival of the Empire, figure-following bodice, producing a smooth line from bust to hips, but making the most of all curves. This meant that corsets became longer, tighter and more generally constricting. In addition there was a considerable increase of interest in artificial aids for the bosom, which had made their début in the earlier Empire phase of the turn of the century. They abounded from this time. In 1860 a patent had been obtained for 'an improved inflated undulating artificial bust' to augment the female figure – a description which suggests that there had been previous versions of a similar kind. In 1867 a French firm advertised *poitrines adhérentes* of pink rubber, which were described as 'following the movements of respiration with mathematical and perfect precision'. Other similar devices followed in continuous succession, including numerous styles and sizes of bust pads, celluloid and rubber bust shapes and 'lemon bosoms', round about this period.

The *cuirasse* bodice was the name given to the style which evolved in

81 Bustles of 1872, made of horsehair and dimity

During the age of bustles 1870s

82 Corsets of 1880, with high busts and long fronts

IZOD'S PATENT CORSETS.

TRADE MARK

TRADE MARK

PEAR   BUSK

FIGURE

REGULATOR.

DIEU·ET·MON·DROIT

These Corsets may be had of all respectable Drapers and Ladies' Outfitters, at various prices, and in a the 1870s and that is just what it was. Tight lacing was carried to extremes, and to this period belong some of the most eloquent arguments on the subject, conducted in magazine articles and also in whole books by doctors, reformers and fashion followers. One of the most extraordinary was a fervent and highly coloured defence of tight lacing, *The Corset and the Crinoline*, by W.B.L. (William Barry Lord), published in 1868 and the subject of considerable attention. Although sub-titled 'A book of modes and costumes from remote periods to the present time', its main purpose was to justify tight lacing in all its rigours and to defend 'the stays by the aid of which . . . wives and daughters are made presentable to society'. Arguments are piled upon arguments to produce a Pelion-upon-Ossa proof that from prehistory the hour-glass figure has been approved and that it is not harmful. A letter from *The Queen* is quoted, urging blandly that 'if the various organs are prevented from taking a certain form or direction, they will accommodate themselves to any other with perfect ease'. The prolonged correspondence in the *Englishwoman's Domestic Magazine* on tight lacing at the end of the 1860s, under the aegis of Samuel Beeton, is now accepted as spurious and 'porn', with its sadistic descriptions of tight lacing and flagellation appealing to the prurient and the pervert – and presumably increasing sales thereby.

But were corsets all that bad and was tight lacing so drastic? A revealing footnote to these and a host of other accounts of the subject has been given in our time by Doris Langley Moore, a leading costume expert. In order to find out the facts about the reputed 18-inch waist she measured more than 1,000 waisted women's costumes from the Victorian period. She failed to find any less than 20 inches round the waist. The Gallery of Costume at Manchester bears out her findings: it has no dress on show that measures less than 21 inches at the waist.

At the beginning of the 1880s the bustle came back again, in even more exaggerated forms than those of a decade previously. The fashionable outline now showed a large horizontal projection at the back, usually supported not only by back flounces on the petticoat but also by a larger than ever separate 'basket' of whalebone, cane or steel attached to the waist between the petticoat and dress. It was known as a crinolette. 'The crinoline projected hideously at the side, whereas the crinolette will only stick out at the back', commented *The World* in 1881. It was even said that a tea-tray could be laid safely on this projection, so wide did it sometimes become. With this contraption the dress was still pulled tightly back across the figure from waist to knee, often with tapes.

In the 1880s corsets were longer. The spoon busk appeared and great numbers of whalebones were used. One of these of the early 1880s has 20 separate shaped pieces and 16 whalebones on each of its two sides.

The elegance of corsets increased and the skill put into their construction encouraged dressmakers to shape skirts more closely than ever to the figure. Corsets were often coloured, with gold, Cambridge blue, navy and amber as favourite hues. Most, however, were in white, black or grey. For the fashionable, there were corsets of satin, lace-edged. To keep the bones in position embroidery was frequently used: some of the patterns still survive.

The variety of bustles was immense and they were widely advertised and had special names. One at least, which seemed in name at any rate to be in line with a coming trend in outer clothing and underwear, was described in an advertisement as 'the braided wire health bustle, warranted to be less heating to the spine than any others'. Health had not hitherto been a pre-requisite of underwear. Lillie Langtry gave her name to another bustle of the time, described by James Laver as 'an arrangement of metal bands working on a pivot. It could be raised when sitting down and sprang back automatically when the lady rose to her feet! One of the most extraordinary inventions in the whole history of fashion'.

Petticoats became increasingly elaborate and also became extremely

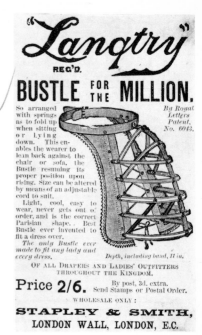

83   A famous bustle of 1877, named after Lillie Langtry

84   Bustles galore of the 1880s

colourful. A fashion book produced by Debenham & Freebody for the autumn in 1874 states, in notes relating to underclothing, that 'In Petticoats one of the best patterns for day wear has a deep kilted flounce all round, wheels of embroidery appearing on the outside of each plait; it has the advantage of ironing easily. For evening wear they are made very long and elaborately trimmed with plaitings, lace and embroidery. There are various new arrangements of stiff skirts for evening wear. Among the best are those made in check muslin, buttoning down the front and having a series of flounces at the back, under the two upper ones of which are tape runners that draw them together, and make them more bouffante. In addition to this, a double puff of the cross-cut muslin, is made to button on at the waist, so as to iron more easily.

'The washing steel suitable for all climates', the book continues, 'is a spécialité to be highly recommended. The newest Crinolettes from Paris are made of red Cashmere, they button down the front, but have only steels at the back; their peculiar feature being, that, in addition to the usual steels in tape-runners, they have outside these a series of red Cashmere flounces edged with steel'.

These are awe-inspiring details, but there was no end to the elaborations of the petticoats of the last twenty years of the nineteenth century. A pink satin petticoat of the 1880s is more than four yards wide at the hem, above which it is lined and stiffened. Deep folds at the back draw the fullness there. All but the main seams are hand-sewn, including all the frills. A purple satin quilted petticoat of the same time has similar back pleats. Another is in quilted Paisley pattern, and one in black taffeta has a long train and is entirely hand-sewn. All these are included in the Museum of Costume at Bath.

In addition to quilted petticoats for warmth, many were made of flannel. Red flannel came to the fore in 1880, and was 'believed to have some special efficacy in keeping out chills, and the most elegant as well as the humblest women wore it', but it was used prior to that. A red flannel crinoline with four steel hoops is included in the collection at Snowshill Manor.

About this time the Princess petticoat appeared, named after Princess Alexandra. Combining camisole or bodice and petticoat in a one-piece garment and originally buttoning down the back, it was a tribute to the beautiful and elegant wife of the heir to Victoria's throne. The Princess was, however, not the inventor of it, any more than Wellington invented the boot called after him. (But Lillie Langtry, the Jersey Lily, did start the fashion for the woven material known ever since as jersey. Also Lord Cardigan, after standing with his back to the fire and burning his coat tails, cut off the tails and thereby introduced the casual short jacket which was henceforth to be called after him.

85   Red flannel petticoat of 1880s with shaped yoke in natural coloured cotton

Lord Raglan originated the sleeve called after him and Lord Spencer was the source of the spencer).

An important innovation at this time was the first suspender. James Laver records that in 1876 Grand Opéra Bouffe, with music by Offenbach, was presented at the Alhambra Theatre, Leicester Square, and great excitement was roused by French dancers with 'naked thighs with suspenders stretched across them to keep up the stockings'. By 1878 these suspenders were being worn in Britain in real life. They were originally attached to a separate kind of harness and later to a belt, both worn over the corset, and it was not until 1901 that they were attached to the corset. They were a double boon, not only replacing restricting garters but also anchoring the corset so that it could be

86 (*above left*)   Harness-type suspenders, c.1880

87 (*above right*)   Suspenders on corset belt, c.1886

88   Day dress of 1885, with skirt looped up to show petticoat-like underskirt (from *La Mode Artistique*)

longer and more shapely. Eventually, too, suspenders made it possible for the corset to be less constricting. As they kept it in place and prevented it from riding up, the waist did not have to be so desperately tight in order to achieve this result.

In the early 1880s the bustle, instead of being a waist-high projection, had evolved into a cluster of draped material below the hipline at the back. Above it the dress followed the figure to this point more closely than it had done for centuries. The fullness of petticoats was sometimes pulled away from the front by the further aid of drawstrings. There was, however, a brief return of the high projecting bustle in the later 1880s, when it was combined with a very tight, flat front from throat to hem.

Underwear in general began to be modernised in order to accommodate these styles, but for most of the nineteenth century its main characteristic, and the oddest to our eyes, was its voluminousness. Chemises of the early nineteenth century are huge. They have enormously wide necklines, caught in by drawstrings, and wide sleeves, often also pulled in at the elbow. Frequently there were additional pieces inserted at the top of the sleeves, and these were flattened by minute pleating given to them in the ironing. The sleeve was still a straight piece of material with a large under-arm gusset to make movement possible.

Typical good quality chemises of the mid-nineteenth century are made of extremely fine linen, almost of a handkerchief-like texture. The sewing, still, of course, by hand, is meticulously fine and impeccably neat, both inside and out. The size of the garments, the amount of elaboration in the cutting of sleeves and yokes and the extent of fine tucking make them remarkable. One young lady is on record as having spent a month sewing and embroidering one undergarment.

From the 1860s chemises started to become more attractive. Broderie anglaise was used to edge the neck and sleeves, which were shorter. Later in the century lace edging and rows of lace insertion appeared. Sleeves sometimes were absent, the armholes being finished by a row of lace or broderie anglaise. Necklines became less wide and the tighter neck was fastened by means of a button on a short front opening. Sometimes the garments became rather shorter – above knee-length – but for many years after the half-century they were still immensely wide and often long enough to reach the calves of the average woman. By the mid-seventies the chemise was being shaped to the waist below the bust, so as to make it less bulky and conform to the flatter line of waist and hips in outer clothes.

It is a curious fact that the Victorians, usually regarded as a byword for dreary practicality in underwear, were in fact innovators in the introduction of finer materials, trimmings of lace and embroidery and were also the first to introduce silk as an underwear material. This was in the 1880s. 'Underclothing is now made in soft silk and is as much trimmed with lace as our dresses, with hand embroidery most beautifully done,' said *Sylvia's Home Journal* in 1880. By the end of the century wool was worn for warmth, but for fashion, 'fine lawn, muslin and silk, trimmed with lace and embroidery and threaded with ribbons, had become still more decorated and more decorative' says Anne Buck, an authority on Victorian costume.

Drawers were by the 1880s in general wear, and they shared with chemises the outstanding property of being enormous in size. Examples in the collection at the Victoria and Albert Museum give the impression, as do the chemises, of being made for giantesses. They are two or three times as large as would seem necessary or desirable.

89　Knee-length cotton chemise edged with eyelet embroidery, *c.*1866

The design of drawers, from the 1860s until the early years of the twentieth century, still consists of two almost separate sections, one for each leg, joined only just below the waist, where they are gathered on to a substantial band. They are therefore open from below-waist to the edge of the leg. Sometimes drawers are cut entirely on the cross, at others large godets are added to the opening at the back, so that the two sides can overlap voluminously. These garments usually fasten at the waistband, crossing over at the back, with tapes going round the waist to secure them.

One example at the Victoria and Albert Museum carries the monogram VR and belongs to the 1860s. It has the usual open back and the waistband has tapes which cross over at the back. The legs are straight, with rows of minute tucks to decorate them. The material is very fine linen and the sewing is so minute as to be almost invisible.

90　White cotton open drawers with back fastening, *c.*1860

Drawers had become knickers by the 1880s. A writer in *Cassell's Magazine* in 1882 said: 'I recommend flannel knickers in preference to flannel petticoats'. In 1895 *Home Chat* declared: 'We are really most keen over the construction of these knickers, knowing as we do from experience their great comfort'. The same popular weekly in the same year finds that 'the ideal knickers are of black satin, with removable lanura lining', and advises 'serge knickers, for a girl from twelve to sixteen'. In 1926 it mentions French knickers, then a novelty. *Vogue* in the same year describes 'Directoire Knickers of milanese'.

Other drawers which belonged to Queen Victoria were included in a London auction sale in 1977, when a newspaper report said that they 'resembled two great linen slings gaping open at the front and held together by a drawstring'.

About 1877 a new undergarment appeared, the first of a whole series that were to proliferate from then into the following century and in so doing to transform underwear and help to produce an entirely new concept of it. This novelty was combinations. They combined chemise and drawers in one garment and were at first made in the same linen and cotton materials, and also at times of flannel and merino. Their attraction was that they reduced the bulk of the underwear and therefore helped the trend of outer fashion towards bodices that followed the figure closely down to the bottom of the hips – a trend not seen for centuries. The main development of combinations came, however, considerably later and falls mainly into the early part of the present century. But during the last quarter of the nineteenth century they jostled quite actively with the traditional chemise and drawers for a place in the underwear wardrobe.

The cult of slimness, which they would have aided, was not showing any signs of capturing fashion, and the vogue of the times was for the other extreme. The ideal, laid down in 1873 as the taste of the time, declared that 'a well-developed bust, a tapering waist and large hips are the combination of points recognised as a good figure' – and that lasted for more than thirty years, during which the mature beauty with a flamboyant figure reigned supreme, for the last time.

The bust, as at certain previous times and at all periods since then to our own day, was provided with artificial aids to curvaceousness when nature failed. With the lengthening of corsets to ensure becomingly flowing hips, these garments became correspondingly shorter above the waist. The under-bodice or camisole, introduced to cover the gap, and gaining steadily in popularity and elegance, was not an effective shapemaker. There were, however, plenty of additional remedies available.

In addition to the many false busts there were also, in the 1880s, camisole-like garments with elaborate structures of whalebone or a

91   Jaconet under-bodice,
c.1876

92   Bust bodice, boned and
taped to give round effect,
c.1890

93   Heavily boned bust bodice,
c.1890

series of wire springs built into the underside of the front. By adjusting certain tapes these could produce an 'improved' bust of selected dimensions. It was a feature of these that there was a complete absence of any division or of the much-sought-after 'cleavage' of later times. The bust was a rounded bolster, providing, perhaps with more comfort than later, Browning's dream of 'the breast's superb abundance where a man might lay his head'.

These new garments which gave artificial shape to the bust were the first bust bodices, forerunners of an article of underwear which by the early twentieth century was to be one of the most important of all, probably second only to the corset in its contribution to fashion. And though its history covers only about eighty years, it has in that time gone through as many changes and variations as has corsetry in all the centuries.

Nightdresses became increasingly distinguishable from chemises at this time, in that they were made with yokes, collars and cuffs. They were often tucked and trimmed with lace or embroidery. Generally, however, they were still made of white cotton of various types, with a tendency towards finer weaves. Some nightdresses which belonged to Queen Victoria were sold by auction in the autumn of 1977; they were made of fine white linen embroidered with the Royal cyphers. The nightcap, outmoded in the past decade or two, had a brief revival anticipating the boudoir cap to come.

Stockings of the 1880s were coloured again, after varying from black or grey to white, and were often embroidered with clocks, sometimes in contrasting colours, and with motifs embellishing the front from the toes upwards.

94 Stockings of the mid-nineteenth century, with embroidered clocks and fronts and contrasting colours

9

Revolt against Fashion and the banishment of the corset 1850–1880

Throughout the nineteenth century, if appearances alone were considered and the leading fashion magazines regarded as full evidence, fashion was proceeding according to its established pattern, supplying the needs of the well-heeled, the leisured, the class-conscious, bearing in mind the part vanity, sex-appeal and novelty played in making a mode successful.

But behind the scenes a revolution without precedent in the history of fashion was building up in several different directions. Physical health and fitness, bodily comfort and the rational design of garments, both outer and under, were becoming factors of growing importance in what people, and especially women, wore. Previously the well-being and ease of the wearer had had little, if anything, to do either with fashionable dress or with the hidden garments that were the chief shapemakers. Now, however, change was on its way, albeit obscurely, and eventually it was to transform the whole concept and structure of fashion in our own time.

Pleas for comfortable clothes for children had been voiced from at least the Elizabethan age, mainly by schoolmasters and other educationalists. Locke at the end of the seventeenth century and Rousseau, influenced by him almost a century later, had produced some practical results in this area and had laid the foundations of a new kind of thinking about clothes. Women's fashions had been the subject of ridicule and satire, especially in the eighteenth century, with Hogarth and Rowlandson taking the lead in exposing their follies. That fashion could be not only ridiculous but also harmful to health and comfort was, however, a view that had no practical force until the nineteenth century. Attacks on fashion on these grounds were part of the moral zeal and social conscience which, for the first time in known history, pervaded Victorian society, producing new attitudes to the community and a new zeal for reforms of all kinds, which have had a continuous growth and development into the Welfare State of our own time.

As early as 1832 the importance of health factors in dress had been brought forward by Dr Andrew Combe, MD, in his *Principles of Physiology applied to the preservation of Health and to the development of physical Education*. He advocated the dress reform of wearing flannel next to the skin on health grounds and declared that women's clothes in particular were too tight-fitting and therefore injurious to health. He singled out for specific attack the habit of tight lacing, with its distortion of the natural figure: 'Misled . . . by ignorance, and a false and most preposterous taste, women of fashion, and their countless flocks of imitators, down even to the lowest ranks of life, have gradually come to regard a narrow or spider-waist as an ornament worthy of attainment at any cost or sacrifice', he declared. He contrasted this with the beauty of the natural shape of antique statues. His book had run into 14 editions by 1852, so it evidently was widely read, though not followed by fashion at that time. Unfortunately he did not propose an alternative form of dress and Mrs Bloomer's suggested solution of 1851, which endeavoured to do so, was too drastic to succeed at the time.

Surprisingly, the first constructive revolt against corsets and petticoats, which were mainly responsible for fashion's distortions, came from the world of art. Its source was the Pre-Raphaelite Brotherhood, formed in 1848 by John Millais, William Holman Hunt and Dante Gabriel Rossetti. The aim of the group was to bring art in a wide sense, not just painting, back to nature and to free it from the outworn, stereotyped, academic conventions which they believed were inhibiting it at the time. Many held that the departure from its true course had started in Raphael's time. Involved in this movement was admiration for the soft, unrestricting lines of female dress as seen in medieval paintings, illustrations and other surviving reproductions, especially those of the reign of Edward III. Loose, flowing gowns, falling from the shoulders, slackly girdled at the natural waist and often with wide sleeves, were their ideal. At the time such dress, wholly different from the current plethora of fashionable petticoats and tight bodices with tighter waists, was worn only by the women closely linked to the P.R.B. circle, among them Rossetti's model, Elizabeth Siddal, his sister the poetess Christina, and Jane Morris, all of whom are seen in dress of this relaxed style, in sketches, paintings and photographs of the time of the crinoline.

The keynote of this type of dress was liberation – from the trammels of the corset and also from the dictates of changing fashion, against both of which Pre-Raphaelite or aesthetic dress, as it came to be called, was firmly set. But it took some 20 years and the widening of the original artistic movement by a link-up with the social, or socialist thinking

95   Aesthetic dress in a portrait by Dante Gabriel Rossetti

of William Morris, plus the growth of the women's movement, to bring such dress into a degree of prominence and acceptance. It remained, even then, a minority movement, out of the mainstream of fashion, but sowing seeds which were to come to fruition in the twentieth century.

By the 1870s the rise of aesthetic dress was sufficiently important for *The Queen*, then as now a recorder of socially acceptable fashion, to commission three articles on it from Eliza Mary Haweis, a prolific and well-established journalist, costume historian and pioneer of women decorators, on the subject. She moved in artistic circles and was a strong individualist in dress, though it is unlikely that she followed the aesthetic styles strictly. In her books, *The Art of Beauty* and *The Art of Dress*, published in 1878 and 1879 respectively, she put forth the theory of the P.R.B. on dress: 'The primary rule in a beautiful dress is that it shall not contradict the natural form of the human frame. . . . One of the most important features in a graceful figure . . . is the waist. The first aim is to have an "antique waist" – which a vulgar mind would pronounce horribly thick – thick like the Venus de Medicis, thick like that of the far nobler Venus de Milo'.

The 'antique waist' was the main feature of aesthetic dress, and it hit straight out at the cherished corset. It had to be completely un-trammelled and in the natural place. 'The first aim of the Pre-Raphael-ite woman', says Alison Gernsheim, 'was to have an "antique waist" rather broad and in the natural position'. No corset of that or previous times had had this as its aim.

This cult was followed mainly by artistic and intellectual women who were hostile to the extravagances of conventional fashion and found here a welcome relief from it. The novelist E. Nesbit was a fervent follower, much given to large and shapeless garments, a non-corset wearer who also cut her hair short. She bought strange coloured tweeds in profusion, for clothes for herself and her daughters, and thus contributed to the 'greenery-yallery' side of the aesthetic cult. Char-lotte Yonge described aesthetic dress in her novels.

During the rise of the aesthetic movement there appeared a book which was a broadside directed against fashion, mainly on health grounds. This was *Madre Natura versus The Moloch of Fashion. A Social Essay*, by Luke Limner (John Leighton). Published in 1874, it sets out 'to portray the pernicious effects of a grand social error', that is, tight lacing and other fashions, and it received considerable atten-tion. From a general attack on the evils of fashion, including the deaths by burning caused by the crinoline, it goes on to concentrate on the distortion of the body produced by tight stays, illustrated by drawings of contorted skeletons. He pleads for this subject to be treated more seriously, quotes attacks on fashion made by philosophers and aesthetic writers and ends fearsomely by ascribing no fewer than 97 diseases to the wearing of tight corsets and stays! But while attacking current and past fashions, he, like Dr Combe, does not suggest any alternatives.

The keynote of this stage of the revolt against fashion was liberation – from the all-confining corset above all and from the dictates of changing fashions, against which Pre-Raphaelite or aesthetic dress was equally firmly set. The 'antique waist' meant that its wearers threw away their corsets. This was a much more dramatic and drastic challenge to fashion than the reputed burning of bras by the liberated women of the 1960s, who had a century or more of progressing emancipation to support them even if their bras didn't. Even in the 1870s it meant a complete breakaway from the fashionable figure and from the accepted panoply of underwear of the time.

So far the change was mainly aesthetic in its motivations, based on the belief that only what was natural could be beautiful, but there was a close association of ideas between this and the concurrent development of the movement for the improvement of the status of women and their attainment of personal freedom and political recognition. The latter had gone far enough for John Stuart Mill, a firm supporter, who in 1861 had advocated women's suffrage in his book *Representative Government*, to propose a form of enfranchisement of women in an amendment to the Representation of the People Act of 1867. Although defeated it secured the votes of 81 MPs.

But in general fashion's conventions were accepted. One main reason was that the pioneers of women's rights were aware that their demands would be regarded by the majority of men and women as an enormity. They themselves would therefore be expected to look freakish in dress. As this would obscure their real purpose they made it almost a point of honour to conform strictly to the fashions of their time. When a special meeting of the Social Science Association, a liberal organisation founded by F.D. Maurice and favouring women's emancipation, was held in 1866 during the campaign to give girls the

96   Rational dress, as seen at the Exhibition of Hygienic Costume, 1882

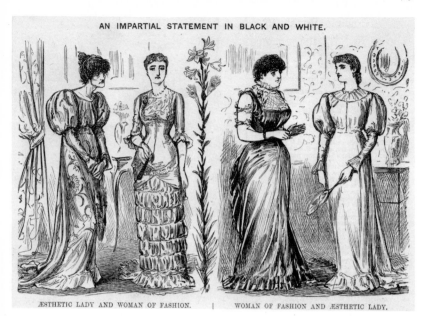

AN IMPARTIAL STATEMENT IN BLACK AND WHITE.

ÆSTHETIC LADY AND WOMAN OF FASHION. | WOMAN OF FASHION AND ÆSTHETIC LADY.

97 Aesthetic dress versus Fashion, 1881

right to take the Oxford and Cambridge Local Examinations, Miss Emily Davies, a pioneer of the women's movement, made special arrangements for 'some well-dressed and good-looking young women to fill up the front row', in order to refute the idea of frumpish blue-stockings. When, in the 1870s, women were undertaking the pioneer activity of addressing public meetings all over Britain in support of the parliamentary vote for women, it was noted that 'when an audience expected to find a fierce and strident virago, and found instead a young lady whose voice, dress and manner were not only quiet but exquisite, then indeed they were startled to attention'. When the first women students were admitted to Oxford, there was great anxiety that they should 'dress carefully and have gentle manners', and the rules of chaperonage were followed as strictly as in the conventional society of the time.

That dress reform should be a top priority in the emancipation of women was, however, the belief of one vigorous group. Amelia Bloomer's effort of 1851 had failed dismally, but in 1880 the Rational Dress Society, led by Lady Harberton, was established and proceeded to promote the cause of health, comfort and sense in dress, and especially in women's dress. It condemned tight lacing, high heels, all the garments which cramped movement. It objected to all types of crinolines and crinolettes. It omitted corsets from its list of approved underwear, including only a firm bodice to support the bust and provide anchorage for garments fastening round the waist. It specified that the total weight of underwear should not exceed 7 lbs – a weight that would be intolerably heavy by today's standards. It disapproved of

98   Aesthetic dress, 1882, from a *Punch* drawing by Charles Keene

changes in fashion, considering that its criterion of health, comfort and beauty precluded the constant eddies of change which had typified fashion – not only fashion in dress – for centuries. It was the first outright anti-fashion – or it tried to be.

The Rational Dress Society voiced its views in its own publication, which started in 1888 and gave considerable support to the idea of divided skirts, but of a loose Turkish style, not mannish trousers. The *Gazette*, as it was called, seems to have faded away in 1889, but the Society continued to campaign for a time.

One peak of the health cult which affected clothing was the great International Health Exhibition of 1884, popularly known as 'The Healtheries'. It was a fantastic show, with Queen Victoria as its patron and the Prince of Wales its president, and it occupied an immense site on which stand most of the present South Kensington Museums. It extended from Kensington Gore to Cromwell Road and from Exhibition Road to Queen's Gate. It attracted attendances of 4,167,683 people between its opening on 8 May and its extended closing date of 30 October.

The dress section was 'illustrated chiefly in its relation to health' and the Eastern Side Gallery, said the catalogue, 'contains a collection of ladies' underclothing designed specially with reference to hygienic considerations. Naturally, improved corsets of numerous patterns form a large feature in this Exhibition. There are also some comparatively novel and very beautiful materials, such as crêpe and net for underclothing, silk longcloth, and a pine-wool fabric, which is said to protect the body against rheumatism'.

Crinolines, it is noted, are 'ridiculous and we have only been saved from a renewed invasion of them within the past few years by the wise veto of ladies in high places, without whose patronage no change in costume can ever ripen into fashion'. That makes strange reading today.

The campaign for freedom in dress continued, and was voiced again in 1893 in *Aglaia*, the ambitiously produced but short-lived publication of a new reforming body concerned with the dress of both men and women, the Healthy and Artistic Dress Union, founded in 1890. Its interests ranged over a vast area of reform, from vegetarianism to the William Morris kind of socialist thinking about the working classes. The aim of *Aglaia*, however, was 'the propagation of sound ideas on the subject of dress', its title was the name of one of the three classical graces, the one whose sphere was adornment, but 'we seek the aid of all the graces', and 'the signs are many that the educated world is endeavouring to introduce beauty into its daily life'. *Aglaia*'s three numbers, the last of them appearing in 1894, included an article on the harm done by corsets, by Dr Wilberforce Smith, which admitted that corset-wearing was 'about as widely spread as the habits of civilisation and about as old as civilisation'. The last number had advertisements for 'Athenian Gowns' and 'Hygienic knickers'. These were Capper's 'Csando' Hygienic knickers, cut 'so as to admit of perfect freedom to the body either Walking, Riding, or Sitting; no strain on any part. It is both warm and comfortable, and all superfluous plaitings and fulness is entirely dispensed with. Made in fine coating cloth of various substances, unlined 15/9, with removable flannel lining 21/9'.

There was also The Substitute for Stays – the 'Platinum anti-corset – fits like a glove, easily washed'. It embodied 'no compression', 'ease of respiration', 'bones out in 10 seconds for washing', had unbreakable 'platinum' bones and with all this was elegant in appearance. A bodice with soft bust sections and front buttoning was also available.

10

The Health Cult
and wool next to the skin
1880 onwards

'Wool next to the skin' was one of the rules of life for a large proportion of the populace from the '80s and '90s of last century until the development of man-made fibres after the Second World War. It is still widely kept. The cult did not creep in haphazardly and the immense effect it had on the underwear of men, women and children was no mere whim of fashion. The man who assailed the centuries-old acceptance of the cotton chemise or shirt, with a limited use of flannel, usually rough and of mixed origin, was Dr Gustav Jaeger, MD, Professor of Zoology and Physiology at the University of Stuttgart, author of a number of books on health culture and originator of Dr Jaeger's Sanitary Woollen System, which made an immense impact on the development of underwear not only in Germany but all over Europe and not least in Britain.

His first book, a collection of essays on health culture, was published in Germany in 1878 and was based on ten years' study of the subject of clothing and its effect on health. He declared that he cured his own chronic ill-health, excess of weight, indigestion and various other ailments by the wearing of wool clothing. This meant that 'stomach, heart, lungs and brain all show greater vitality'. His wife and children also responded to the 'cure' of wool clothing for various ailments and infections. He himself became able to garden for several hours without strain, an activity previously resulting in exhaustion, and a woollen collar cured a hoarse voice which had interfered with 'my chief pleasure in sitting down at home to the piano and singing a song'. Not only was he cured but 'my daughter remarked that my voice sounded plainer and clearer than ever' and later 'my voice had attained an increased compass'.

The principle behind Dr Jaeger's theory was that only animal fibres prevented the retention of the 'noxious exhalations' of the body, retained the salutary emanations of the body which induce a sense of vigour and sound health and ensured warmth and ventilation. But it had to be wool and wool alone that was worn. Even pockets and linings must be of wool. Handkerchiefs were to be woollen ones, hats likewise, and boots had to have wool inserted in them. All bedding had to be of wool.

The impact Dr Jaeger's clothing made in Britain was due to one man. This was Mr L.R.S. Tomalin, manager of a wholesale grocery firm in the City of London. So impressed was he by reading one of Dr Jaeger's books that he secured the sole rights to the use of the Jaeger name, publications and system, patents, trade marks, etc. in Great Britain, with a view to developing the ideas that so impressed him. He even had a huge bonfire in his garden for all the non-woollen clothing and bed-linen possessed by his household. Mr Tomalin forthwith broke away from his previous occupation and on 1 February 1884 started manu-facturing Jaeger clothing, all of it 100 per cent pure wool, in a small way in premises in Fore Street, in the City. The business made rapid progress and in the autumn of 1884 won a gold medal for its stand at 'The Healtheries' – the International Health Exhibition. In October of the same year the venture received the accolade of a long leader page article in *The Times* on the Jaeger idea that we should all wear wool or other animal fibre clothing. 'A new gospel', *The Times* declared, 'has reached us . . . it is a medical theory, based on the close observations of animal life, demonstrated by scientific experiments, and proved by practical experience . . . the evidence in its favour is sufficiently strong and the success achieved so widespread that it is, at least, only right to state the case, leaving the public, in Dr Jaeger's own words, free to examine everything and retain the best'.

In February 1884 the *Lancet* congratulated Dr Jaeger 'on his able and practical recognition of the usefulness of wool as a covering' and in August of that year the *British Medical Journal* referred to the skill of the new adaptation of animal wool 'as a sanitary substitute in articles hitherto manufactured of other materials'. Doctors testified by the hundred to the relief from rheumatism due to the sanitary woollen system.

After this Fore Street became thronged with carriages from the West End. Some of them contained fashionable ladies brought to Jaeger by Oscar Wilde, who was then at the height of his career and who was an ardent disciple of Dr Jaeger. Another enthusiast was George Bernard Shaw, who is recorded in Frank Harris's biography as having walked up Oxford Street in a Jaeger garment – 'a single garment or combin-ation in brown knitted wool, complete from sleeves to ankles, in one piece'. (Shaw said, much later: 'Jaeger did dreadful things in those days'.) This was a literal interpretation of Dr Jaeger's stipulation to the British Company that clothing should be all-wool, close-fitting, made in natural coloured mixed white and brown wools, undyed and un-

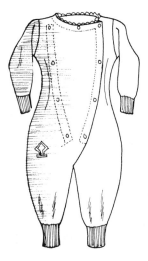

99 Dr Jaeger's sanitary stockinette combinations in pure animal wool with double thicknesses over the chest and stomach, *c*.1886

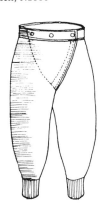

100 Dr Jaeger's woollen stockinette drawers with double front, *c*.1884

101   Dr Jaeger's pure wool corset with back lacing and removable watch-spring steels, c.1886

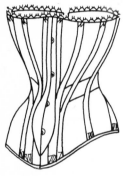

102   Another Jaeger wool corset with spoon busk, c.1886

bleached. The original Jaeger undergarments were 100 per cent pure wool, in the stockinette weave approved by the Doctor on health grounds. They had long sleeves, high necks and were double-fronted, for protection. Typical were combinations, for men, women and children, in summer, winter and winter extra-thick weights.

Women's clothing, including underclothing, engaged considerable attention from Dr Jaeger. 'Here', he says, 'habit and prejudice are even more potent than with men'. And he continues: 'I have to declare war against such cherished finery as silk dresses, white petticoats (often starched so as to make them thoroughly impermeable), linen stays, cotton or silk stockings, and white starched dresses'. What he advocates is that 'chemise, stockings, drawers, petticoat and stays should all be made of pure animal wool. These, with a dress of pure woollen stuff, closing well round the throat, and having a double lining at the chest and downwards, should be the winter and summer wear of women'. On the grounds that women wear too many layers of clothes on the lower half of the body, he elsewhere advises combinations instead of chemise and drawers.

As the corset, at that time tight laced at fashion's behest, was already being attacked on health grounds, it was to be expected that Dr Jaeger would not pass it over. The Sanitary Woollen Corset appeared in the first 1884 catalogues of Jaeger in London and it continued to appear for many years, right into the present century. Dr Jaeger himself refers to attacks on the conventional corset of the time by 'some leading authorities on health culture' and comments: 'the fault does not consist wholly in the wearing of a corset, but partly in the material of which it is made. This is usually substantial (possibly even pasted) linen cloth, and (1) concentrates, in an intensified degree, the disadvantages of clothing made from vegetable fibre; (2) is, as a rule, laced too tightly, because the great enervation of the body, caused by wearing this most unhealthy material, induces a feeling of want of support and a tendency to unshapely increase of bulk, only to be restrained by the use of force, under which the internal organs suffer.

'Ladies, however, who have adopted, and especially those who have grown up under, the Sanitary Corset, need to use no force in order to preserve the shape; their compact, firm figures will not require support. They do not therefore lace too tightly, and in the Sanitary Woollen Corset they have all the advantages of girded loins without the disadvantages'.

The 1884 'sanitary woollen, spring corsets' were described as 'flexible, elastic, durable, with watch spring steels' and as responding to every movement of the body. The steels were buttoned in at the upper end, so that they could be removed for cleaning. The corsets were made in undyed sheep's wool, in white and grey and in camel hair.

Drawers, chemises and petticoats also appear in the 1884 catalogues, and there is a picture of 'sanitary stockinet combinations'. In 1887 a patent stocking suspender, a belt with the suspenders attached, was introduced and was one of the earliest examples of this device to get rid of the constricting garter.

The association of wool with Dr Jaeger was so strongly established that the compilers of the Oxford Dictionary wanted to include his name in one of their editions as meaning any pure wool. At the time of Queen Victoria's first jubilee Jaeger were doing excellent business, 'for then her foreign and colonial visitors all drive up to our shop in royal carriages', according to the recollections of an old employee.

But even in the underwear world fashion never stays still. The pure wool corsets remained until the second decade of this century, following the longer-hipped lines of other corsetry of the time. But by the '30s they were being advertised as 'specially recommended for nurses and invalids'. Children's staybands and corsets also provided a useful side-line.

But the general styling of women's Jaeger underwear moved away from the principles laid down by the good Doctor. By 1913 combinations were being made finely ribbed and in white, with short sleeves and buttoned-up fronts. In 1915 there was 'something quite new' – a crossover bust bodice in white wool taffeta, and also camisoles. By the '30s fashion had won. What would Dr Jaeger have made of the advertisement of the 'vivacious pantie', showing a girl doing the splits in a brief pantie and a shoulder-strapped vest? In the early 1930s the Company was making 'the world's most serene underneaths', including opera vests and panties, and a little later there were 'spring-knit undies' of pure silk and wool, and silk alone, in fashionable peach, pink and white.

In the same year the Company stated that 'we found after a time that people were inclined to think that health clothing might be ugly. Now Jaeger is known to be the reverse; in fact we are leaders today in smart underwear and outerwear'. In 1933 the Company's house magazine recorded that 'Miss Gertrude Lawrence bought a large outfit of frocks and beach-wear at Oxford Street to take away on her summer holiday. So did Miss Madelaine Carroll'. Not, however, of wool.

Dr Jaeger found a loyal and effective supporter, especially where women's underwear was concerned, in Miss Ada S. Ballin, a prominent writer on dress and hygiene in the 1880s and a lecturer to the Rational Dress Society. Her best-known book, *The Science of Dress in Theory and Practice*, published in 1885, referred in its preface to the many books and pamphlets on dress in relation to health which had recently been published, 'the majority having met with indifferent success, perhaps owing to the fact that they have been written *for* women *by*

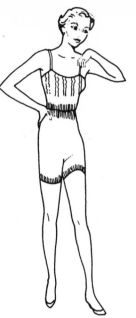

103   Jaeger fine ribbed wool combinations, 1913

104   Jaeger combinations in wool crêpe, trimmed with lace and ribbon, and with wide French legs, 1917

105   Jaeger vest and pantie in pure wool, 1935

106   Jaeger silk cami-knickers, 1938

men who obviously have not well been able to enter into the feelings and conditions of their readers, nor to speak from personal experience'. She takes a middle of the road position on dress reform, endeavouring 'to point out how clothing may be made, as far as possible, healthy without being unfashionable'. Hygienic clothing, she says, is widely advertised, but much of it has no claim to the description. She herself, she says, has arranged for certain firms to make clothes under her direction.

'The battle of dress reform is at the present time being vigorously fought', she claims. She urges the wearing of pure wool, to absorb the 'noxious exhalations' of the skin, so prominent in Dr Jaeger's gospel of health, which were such a cause for concern at the time. Woollen combinations, she urges, should be worn, but over them as few garments as possible. The chemise can be dispensed with and sensible girls, she notes, wear combinations, stays and just one petticoat. She condemns the 'baneful practice of tight lacing'. Stays should be made of woollen material and 'good staymakers should be employed. . . . The Cotton stays, sold by the Rational Dress Society, are to be recommended for ladies who are not inclined to corpulence'; others should wear stiffer stays.

She traces drawers back to early in the century, in Court and other fashionable circles – the 'upper ten thousand'. They were, she says, introduced 'when, owing to Royal example, the fashion of distending the skirts with hoops was universally adopted alike by Princess and peasant girl, this distention of the petticoats made it absolutely necessary to cover women's legs'. Actually the need for coverings came earlier, in the turn-of-the-century vogue for transparent dresses which also called for concealment of the legs. Of the Bloomer fashion Miss Ballin comments that 'though it had many good points about it, it represented too violent a change from the fashions of the time, and ladies would not adopt it for fear of appearing ridiculous'. But ever since then, she notes, the divided skirt had been coming up for discussion and a trouser dress had been shown at the Healtheries.

Miss Ballin devoted a whole chapter of her book to children's dress, arguing that reform should start with the young. When she gave, at the Healtheries, the only lecture devoted to dress she chose children's attire as her subject, urging, as zealously as Dr Jaeger, the importance of all-over, cover-up garments in the interests of health.

By a curious coincidence only four years after Dr Jaeger's 'sanitary woollen system' had been launched in Britain in 1884 with immediate success, there came another innovation in underwear fabrics which made an almost comparable impact upon traditional undergarments worn by men, women and children.

One great merit of wool, according to Dr Jaeger, was its porousness. This he denied to cotton and all other materials not of animal origin, but he was soon to be challenged. Late in 1887 the idea of cellular materials was first thought of and in the following year Aertex came into existence. It is still, like Jaeger, a household word and in many ways it has remained even closer to its original conception.

Aertex, like wool, was associated with the health cult of the time. The originator of it was Mr Lewis Haslam, for many years MP for Newport, Mon. The scene of the invention was a sanatorium at Westward Ho, Devon, where, along with Mr Haslam, were staying two notable members of the medical profession, Sir Benjamin Ward Richardson and Dr Richard Greene.

Mr Haslam's starting point was a belief in the value of fresh air. Fresh air should not only be breathed into the lungs but should respirate the skin. It could, he believed, not only have a positive effect on health but also insulate the body against heat and cold. The idea had originally stemmed from a discussion about the warmth which was promoted by wool when it was new and fluffy and therefore contained air, but which ceased to be effective when wool was washed and became felted, as was almost unavoidable in those days.

What was wanted therefore was a material that would continue to hold air through many wearings and washings. Cotton was the answer. Its absorbency would ensure the retention of its stable form. The need was simply to find a weave that provided aerating qualities.

Mr Haslam carried his two famous medicos with him in this belief and in March 1888 the Aertex Company was set up in a small office in Aldermanbury for the purpose of manufacturing cellular fabrics. Sir Benjamin was chairman and the two other members of the pioneering trio were among the directors. At first only the materials were produced. The new company concentrated its efforts on promoting the idea of the revolutionary fabric with holes in it and on selling Aertex materials to clothing and underclothing manufacturers. The enterprise was a success and the idea of a fabric that would not only be cooler in summer but also warmer in winter caught on so firmly that by November 1889 larger premises were needed. To start with, men's clothing alone was made but in 1891, when Aertex started making up its own garments, the women's underwear market was broached for the first time. This was in another new factory in Gresham Street 'staffed' by one treadle machinist and one finisher. By January 1892 there was a move to Fore Street (where Jaeger also had its premises) and by then there were ten machinists and six other employees.

From this time expansion went on steadily, with a second factory at Swindon in 1901 and consolidation of manufacture at Nottingham some years later. Cellular materials increased in variety and scope. The Victoria and Albert Museum has a pair of white Aertex combinations of the early 1900s. Very utilitarian, they are reinforced with tapes at the darted waist, buttoned all down the front, but trimmed with broderie anglaise at the neck, sleeves and knee-length legs. Today women's

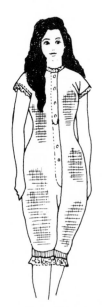

107 Aertex vest, 1889   108 Aertex combinations, 1894   109 Aertex corset, c.189[

Aertex underwear is styled in line with fashion and the market for it continues to be an important one, with particular attractions for tropical wear, where the newer synthetics are not satisfactory.

Another underwear fabric that made its mark in the development of materials with health attributes was Viyella. Produced by William Hollins & Co after long experiments in blending wool and cotton in satisfactory proportions and in the best methods of weaving a fabric, Viyella came on the market in a small way in 1891 as a fabric for men's shirts and nightshirts, but clothes for women and children were soon being made. In 1894 it became the first fabric to carry a registered trade mark. As the twentieth century brought a powerful swing over from made-to-order underclothing to ready-made garments, Viyella started manufacturing its own garments instead of simply selling the material to manufacturers. This side of the business grew rapidly and extensively from the time of the launching of the first season's range of undergarments in the autumn of 1904. Today Viyella in both woven and knitted underwear and outer garments is as much a household name as it ever was, and, like Jaeger and Aertex, it has become invested with a fashion quality that has enlivened its character and enlarged its scope. In addition it has maintained its original claim, very noteworthy at the time, that 'Viyella does not shrink', surmounting with vigour a crisis in 1911 when the increasing use of laundries had produced evidence that the claim was vulnerable to new-fangled machine methods.

110 Aertex vest and knickers, 1938

The biggest influence of all in the transformation of women's underwear in the nineteenth century came, as often happens in history, not by the concentrated conscious efforts of political, social or health reformers but by something else that arrived right out of the blue. It was the bicycle which, as Dr C.W. Cunnington observed with masterly brevity and completeness, 'converted the lady into a biped and supplied her with a momentum which carried her headlong into the next century'. The original 'penny-farthing' of 1871 had been unmanageable by anyone except a long-legged man, but the safety bicycle, which was introduced in 1885, was widely adopted by both men and women within a few years. The introduction of the pneumatic tyre by Dunlop in 1888 was an additional incentive, and by the early '90s women had taken up cycling with fervour. Fashionable ladies even drove to the park in their carriages complete with bicycles which were unloaded for a ride when the open spaces were reached. Bloomers and various styles of divided skirts and knickerbockers naturally sprang into fashion and for sport at least dress was becoming 'rational', though slowly.

In 1893 Ada S. Ballin in *Health and Beauty in Dress* advised that women cyclists should wear 'neat dark cloth costumes lined with woollen material, and the ideal way of wearing them is with woollen combinations next the skin, a flannel body (bodice) fitting closely to the

III   Aertex combinations, 1938

figure to take the place of stays, and buttoned to this a pair of knicker-bockers or trousers of cloth to match the dress. Of course, these un-mentionables do not show, but a lady clothed in this way is better able to face the risk of an accident than one in petticoats'.

Bloomers had an uphill fight to secure recognition, and it was often recommended that they should be worn with a skirt, long or knee-length, so that they wavered between being underwear and outerwear. They were often known as 'rationals' and were criticised on the grounds of inelegance but applauded for their comfort and freedom. By about 1896 they were being worn on their own, without skirts but with hip-length jackets. An alternative, which found considerable favour, was a divided skirt, designed with a pleated frill at the hem, to disguise the separation.

Women engaged in so many sports during the nineteenth century that it is astonishing how slow the contemporary enveloping and restricting fashions were to give way to functional clothes, both under and outer, which allowed for freedom of movement. It was not until the turn of the century that a real advance was made. Up to then women played cricket, hockey, golf and tennis, fished, skated, went shooting, climbed mountains, even went ski-ing either in ankle-length skirts, bloomers, divided skirts or skirts looped up fishwife style on to a deep waistband, over bloomers or knickerbockers. In the 1860s they had even gone climbing in crinolines and in the 1870s they crossed glaciers in ankle-length skirts. The chief concession modern progress made to their apparel was that the wearing of woollen combinations and other woollen undergarments of a more or less functional design was universally advocated by writers on the subject. But the idea of discarding corsets was still far from being generally acceptable. In the *Jubilee Graphic* of 20 June 1887 there is an advertisement for 'Brown's Patent "Dermathistic" Corset, Bones, Busks and Steels protected by leather', with the recommendation that 'Ladies who indulge in such healthful and exhilarating exercises as Rowing, Riding, Driving, Lawn Tennis &c. will find the "D" invaluable, the leather being a sure prevention against Bones, Busks and Steels breaking whilst it renders the Corset most delightfully comfortable'.

II

Lingerie and Luxury
1890–1908

The various movements for dress reform in the latter part of the nine-teenth century did not have a material effect upon the mainstream of fashion, although that was what they aimed to do. Summing up in 1895, Mrs Douglas, in her widely read *The Gentlewoman's Book of Dress*, said of the aesthetes: 'Their model for a dress seemed a sack, tied round the waist with a string, with two smaller sacks for sleeves, tied at intervals with more strings. Their hats were modelled on cabbage leaves'. She admitted, however, that while 'the aesthetic movement is past and over, . . . we shall never be quite so crude and tasteless in our colours as before the days of the lily-worshippers'. She allowed that 'the movement in favour of "rational" dress has also taught us much and has effected an astonishing improvement in our underclothing. The adoption of woollen under-garments has resulted in a great gain in health, and the simplicity of the articles of underwear now worn contrasts agreeably with the needless complexity of those in use before. . . . These enlightenments are, unfortunately, still confined to the upper classes. . . . It is the poor, who are more exposed to the weather, who really need to learn the benefits of warm, porous, sensible underclothing'. She approves of Dr Jaeger, who 'is doing his best, and is making charming underclothing of bleached wool of a pleasant creamy shade, trimmed with creamy woollen lace'. Of breeches she does not approve: 'How could a mother in knicker-bockers inspire awe in the hearts of her peccant brood?' Neither in theory nor practice does the modern 'mum' want to be an object of awe to her young family, but her general wearing of trousers is one of the few things that have not been blamed for the defects of the permissive society.

How little immediate impact rational dress had made on fashion was shown even more clearly by the fact that in the last years of last century and the first decade of this fashionable underwear took off into a

112 Dress reform had little effect on general fashion, as is seen by this tennis girl of 1886

SWANBILL CORSETS (Regd.)

SWANBILL
Registered Trade Mark.

9TH TYPE OF FIGURE.
A charming Corset, made of fine white Coutil, giving a most graceful figure, V-shaped at the back, for evening wear. Busk 11½ inches.
Price 21s.
It is also a most comfortable Corset for riding.

1ST TYPE OF FIGURE.
A hand-made Corset in White Coutil, modelled for long-waisted graceful figures. An excellent wearing Corset.
Swanbill Busk, 13 inches. Also in a good wearing dark Grey Coutil. The same price.

4TH TYPE OF FIGURE.
"This Corset is designed for ladies who require a good support for a long slight waist. It is made in fine White Coutil, and also in French Grey Coutil, Fanned Pink. The advantage of a Grey Coutil Stay, compared with a Black one, is in its lightness, as the Grey Coutil requires no lining. Straight Busk, 13½ inches.
Price, in White or Grey, 25s.
A selection of Embroidery and Lace Petticoats, from 10s. 6d. to 70s.

10TH TYPE OF FIGURE.
SWANBILL BELT CORSET.
(Registered).
A SPECIALITE FOR EMBONPOINT.
This is a most successful Corset for ladies inclined to embonpoint. It is made in good quality of Coutil, with belt of stout webbing round the bottom of the corset. The adjustable straps and the arrangement of the front bones give great support, and keep the figure well in below the waist. It is made in White, and also in a useful shade of French Grey. Swanbill Busk, 13½ inches.
Price, White or Grey, 21s.

7TH TYPE OF FIGURE.
A charming French Woven Corset, with fine bones, suited for short slight figures, and those who prefer a light make of Corset. It is also found an excellent stay for young ladies budding into womanhood. Swanbill Busk, 10½ inches.
Price 14s. 6d.
The petticoat is of Surat Silk, trimmed Valenciennes Lace.
Price 39s. 6d.

5TH TYPE OF FIGURE.
A fine finished Corset of French Coutil and picked Whalebone, modelled with exceptional care, for ladies of full good figure. The broad Swanbill Busk, 13½ inches, is most effective in keeping in the figure to a graceful outline.
Price, in Black or White, 35s.

6TH TYPE OF FIGURE.
A hand-made Corset of good shape, made of White Coutil. Specially designed for short stout figures. It will be found a most comfortable and good wearing Corset. Swanbill Busk, 11 inches.
Price 14s. 6d.
The same price in Black Satteen.

Key to Swanbill Corsets, illustrating, by 12 types of Figure, the latest fashion, sent Post Free.
"The illustrations show that a separate study is made of each kind of figure, and a special Corset produced calculated to improve and preserve the particular type for which it is designed. Ladies who are looking for a really good fitting Corset at a reasonable price, and who live in the country, will find this key very useful."—*The Lady.*

113 Corsets and underwear of 1891 show styles for different figure types, thus anticipating the future

114 A corset of 1895

fantasy of silk and satin, lace and ribbon, such as had never been seen before. Luxury and extravagance ran riot, with silks and satins, lace and embroidery contributing to an underwear scene where petticoats could cost £50 apiece.

Lucile, Lady Duff Gordon, the first Englishwoman to achieve an international reputation in the couture world, who was at the height of her career at the start of the 1900s, claimed to have pioneered this opulence of underwear and in her memoirs, published in 1932, gave a highly coloured description of this transformation in the fashionable Edwardian woman's underwear:

'I was particularly anxious to have a department for beautiful underclothes, as I hated the thought of my creations being worn over the ugly nun's veiling or linen-cum-Swiss embroidery, which was all the really virtuous woman of those days permitted herself. . . . I vowed to change all that, and made plans for the day of chiffons and laces, of boudoir caps and transparent nightdresses. . . . So I started making underclothes as delicate as cobwebs and as beautifully tinted as flowers, and half the women in London flocked to see them, though they had not the courage to buy them at first. . . . They all wanted to wear them, but they were not certain of their ground. Slowly they came over to them. . . . Slowly one by one they slunk into the shop in a rather shamefaced way and departed carrying an inconspicuous parcel which contained a crêpe de Chine or a chiffon petticoat and – the majority came back to order more'.

She prospered and, reviewing her success, she declared: 'I was a pioneer, I loosed upon a startled London, a London of flannel under-clothes, woollen stockings and voluminous petticoats, a cascade of chiffons, of draperies as lovely as those of Ancient Greece, of softly rounded breasts (I brought in the brassière in opposition to the hideous corset of the time) and draped skirts which opened to reveal slender legs'.

These claims were exaggerated and some, like others made else-where in her book, were untrue. Silk underwear already existed and silk stockings had a history that went back at least to Elizabethan days. Nor did Lucile invent the brassière. Not for nothing was she the sister of romantic novelist Elinor Glyn. But her fashion era was the one when glamorous underwear first became an important component of fashion, as it has been ever since, and also the era when it had its first heyday of luxury and extravagance.

It was also the era when it was first promoted for those of moderate means as well as for the leaders of fashion. When, in 1902, Mrs Eric Pritchard's *The Cult of Chiffon*, dedicated to her friend Lady Warwick, a famous Edwardian beauty, was published, it too made much of the

115   Corsets of 1900

SWANBILL CORSETS
(Registered).

5th TYPE OF FIGURE.

THE BANDELETTE CORSET.
Price in White £1 5 0
Price in Black............ £1 8 6
Kept in stock in two lengths—for long-waisted and for medium-waisted figures.

SWANBILL BELT CORSET

116 Beautiful lingerie from Liberty, 1905

importance and beauty of underwear. 'The corset of today at its best', she declares, 'is quite the most hygienic and beautiful little garment yet produced, chiefly because there is hardly anything of it'. She says much of 'lace and silken underwear, which is admittedly for the rich', but advises that others should 'get one or two good patterns and give them to a clever needlewoman to be copied in an inexpensive soft white muslin'. Charming nightgowns, she continues, could be acquired also by the not so rich by following a pattern of a good French model. 'Some charming nightgowns of the moment are far from being extravagant. Lots of women nowadays wear silk and find they can pick up really good washing silk at about 2/11 a yard. Now suppose you have a good French model as a pattern you can easily have half a dozen or so made up without a very large expenditure'. After white, pink is recommended as the best washing colour; blue and mauve are apt to fade.

Beautiful underwear, now called lingerie, is regarded by her of great importance. 'Exquisite lingerie forms the foundation of the wardrobe of the woman of refinement', she says, advising that the woman with a dress allowance of 'only' £200 a year (a very considerable amount in those days) should allot one fifth for lingerie and corsets.

High prices are, however, not now necessary, because 'all our best shops nowadays can provide pretty dainty lingerie at moderate prices, although we can, without doubt, easily spend a small fortune on delightful trifles of this description'. She does not question the accepted panoply of many undergarments, but only their character; thus 'the cache-corset, like the chemise, may be a thing of beauty'. She loves it all: 'There is much affinity between a beautiful tea-gown, daintily perfumed lingerie, and a love of art and poetry'. Country underwear troubles her, but she approves of silk or satin knickers, with detachable linings of flannel, linen, or washing silk.

It is a long step away from the reformers, from Miss Ballin, declaring in 1884 at the International Health Exhibition that 'dress should be looked upon from a scientific point of view. It is in truth one of the great powers which preserve or destroy Health, and its influence is increasingly felt from birth to death'. It is also a far way from Harrods' catalogue of 1895, the first to survive, and full of flannelette night-dresses, woollen combinations and other formidable underwear, which remained throughout catalogues of the early 1900s. Immense, tent-like white cotton nightdresses, dated from the 1880s to 1930, comprise the collection of these garments in the Bath Museum of Costume, and though they are often beautifully embroidered and lace-trimmed, they would have horrified Mrs Pritchard. Aesthetic dress also shocked her. It was worn by 'a terrible type', often unwashed, be-draggled and corsetless.

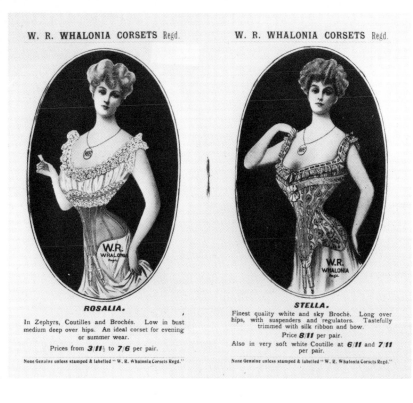

W. R. WHALONIA CORSETS Regd.

W. R. WHALONIA CORSETS Regd.

ROSALIA.

In Zephyrs, Coutilles and Brochés. Low in bust medium deep over hips. An ideal corset for evening or summer wear.

Prices from **3/11½** to **7/6** per pair.

None Genuine unless stamped & labelled " W. R. Whalonia Corsets Regd."

STELLA.

Finest quality white and sky Broché. Long over hips, with suspenders and regulators. Tastefully trimmed with silk ribbon and bow.

Price **8/11** per pair.

Also in very soft white Coutille at **6/11** and **7/11** per pair.

None Genuine unless stamped & labelled " W. R. Whalonia Corsets Regd."

117   The Edwardian corset, with the S-bend, in all its glory, *c.*1905

The luscious, lovely lingerie (invidious to call it underwear) of the fashionable Edwardian lady introduced a new element into the fashion scene and one that has been of importance ever since then. But whatever you call it, underwear needs must be the handmaid of outer fashion, conditioned largely by that fashion. Edwardian fashion still meant an unnatural shape and a restricting one, as the shape of fashion had been throughout its history.

In corsetry there was, however, one curious amalgam of the new luxury look with the increasing concern with health and fitness. A notable innovation in corsetry design had been the 'health' corset, pioneered by Dr Jaeger, as already described. A great number of other designs with similar aims came on the market at the turn of the century.

In late Victorian days Worth, who established the first of the Paris couture houses, was concerned in a movement to introduce a straight-busked health corset and to do away with the figure distortion of the existing style with its tight waist. But the forces which brought the idea into being about 1900 were Dr Franz Glénard and Mme Gaches-Sarraute, whose name is closely associated with the innovation. A corsetière who had studied medicine, she set out to design corsets that would aid health instead of harming or endangering it. She realised the importance of leaving the thorax free yet of supporting the

118   'Gibson Girl' 'S'-shaped corset of 1903–4

119   'Gibson Girl' in white cotton lace and ribbon-trimmed camisole and petticoat, *c.*1903–5

abdomen. She was responsible for the actual introduction of the straight-fronted busk, aimed at supporting and raising the abdomen instead of compressing it and forcing it downwards. By getting rid of the constricting inward curve at the waist, customary in all previous corsets, Madame Gaches-Sarraute aimed at removing pressure on the diaphragm and abdomen and therefore upon vital female organs. Women would at last have room to move and breathe freely and there would be no more harmful compression round and below the waist.

A similar innovation was Carlson's Patent Binder Corset, which was advertised with an impressive list of claims: 'This invention has been submitted by the inventors to the highest medical authorities, both in England and in France, and they unanimously declare that when generally known it will be universally adopted BY ALL CLASSES and entirely supersede the clumsy, heavy corset of the present time. Compression can be regulated to one-sixteenth of an inch, and a perfect figure can be secured while at the same time it materially assists, WITHOUT UNDUE PRESSURE, to obviate the tendency to *embonpoint*'.

Had the purposes of the 'health' corset been achieved it would have been a substantial move towards the production of a corset that would reinforce the natural pull of the muscles between waist and hips and thereby become a valuable health agent. But unfortunately the craze for the small waist persisted. The new health corset was laced up as tightly as its unhealthy forbears, and as a result a new distortion of the figure was created. This was the famous 'S' curve. It was brought about by the fact that if the corset was laced too tightly the new straight busk would push the bust prominently forward and throw the hips back to an extreme degree of physical distortion.

This shape, with lavish bust and impressive hips, conformed to the current ideal of beauty. For the last time between then and now the mature, voluptuous figure with ample curves both at bosom and hips was the fashionable aim. It remained so during the first years of the present century: it accorded well with the Edwardian way of life.

Curves on the bosom were even more important than on the hips, and lack of them was more frequent. The new straight corset could not, like the earlier styles, come high up in front and support or even push up the bust. Its straight line would have made this construction torture, so it left the bust largely unsupported. For this reason and because busts were fashionable, there was an increase in the wearing of various styles of bust bodice and of numerous kinds of bust improvers, from pads and other artificial shapemakers to camisoles with stiffly starched tiers of frills in front to produce an impressive frontage. Edwardian bosoms were worn low, and they overhung the waist, in contrast to the fashions of the mid-twentieth century, which went to the other extreme of 'uplift'. There was as yet no hint at all of cleavage or even of any suggestion of division between the breasts. The female bosom was emphatically bow-fronted.

The epitome of the new figure of fashion was the famous 'Gibson Girl', the exaggerated 'S'-shaped figure immortalised in the drawings of Charles Dana Gibson, the American artist, in the early years of this century and embodied on the London stage by Miss Camille Clifford. The cult reached its peak about 1905.

Surviving undergarments of the early 1900s show how fine silks and light and airy lace had taken over from discreet Victorian linens, lawns and cottons. The whole look was new, yet to us they are period pieces. A pair of combinations of the year 1905, now in the Victoria and Albert Museum Collection, is of the softest and lightest black silk, trimmed with a profusion of very fine écru lace which is slotted through with pink baby ribbon. The legs, still inordinately long and reaching well below any normal knee level, are edged with immense frills of deeply pointed lace. The garment retains the old open style. The legs are almost in two separate pieces, being joined to the top half only at the back of the waist with fine gatherings. There is buttoning all down the front, to a similar opening there from the top of the legs to well down them.

120 Fine black silk combinations trimmed with lace and slotted pink ribbon, c.1905

To the same year, 1905, belongs a pair of black silk knickers (as drawers were now being described) of equal fineness. They carry the fashionable label of Woollands, then located at 2 Lowndes Terrace, SW1 and not on the later Knightsbridge site where the famous fashion store stood until it closed in 1967. These knickers too consist of two almost separate very long leg pieces, and again the only join is at the back of the waist. The fronts are entirely separate, crossing over with fastenings when the garment is put on. There are rows of tiny tucks at the back waistline, and again a profuse amount of lace insertion and frilling edges the wide legs.

121 Matching French knickers in black silk, trimmed with lace and ruching, c.1905

Looking at these examples of fashionable underwear one understands the insistence of the wearers on describing the garments as 'lingerie' for the first time. Nothing comparable had ever before been worn. 'Edwardian underclothes', say the Cunningtons, 'developed a degree of eroticism never previously attempted . . . women had learned much, since the 1870s, of the art of suggestion . . . they invented a silhouette of fictitious curves, massive above, with rivulets of lacy embroidery trickling over the surface down to a whirlpool of froth at the foot'.

It is not surprising that petticoats were advertised at as much as fifty guineas and were made of silk, satin, moiré and various other luxury fabrics. But the opulent look could be secured at a bargain price too, as is shown by a large illustration in a Debenham & Freebody sale catalogue of the early 1900s. It is part of a 'special offer of 1,000 silk

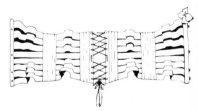

122 1900 pink satin ribbon corset with back lacing and front busk, shows new, lighter design

moirette underskirts, extra rich quality, perfectly fresh, cut in the newest style, extra full, in spots, stripes and chine effects. All colours, extra large and full'. In the picture the petticoat streams out all round with a foaming sea of frilling, ankle-length in front but sweeping the floor at the back, in the prevailing style of fashions of the time. No wonder contemporary fashion journals write of underwear in elaborately emotional and ecstatic terms and always with a degree of solemnity which has never before or afterwards been accorded to the subject. Snobbery was supreme in underwear: when plebeian pink flannelette combinations are mentioned in a ladies' magazine it is stressed that 'we must not call these lingerie'.

It is curious that, parallel to this frou-frou and seductiveness in underwear, there was proceeding the increasing participation of women in sport and other physical activities, for which underwear was of a sober, practical and even formidable kind that ran to the opposite extreme of the fashionable 'frillies'.

Examples of such practical undergarments exist alongside the beguiling 'frillies'. There is, for example, in the Victoria and Albert Museum Collection a very worthy pair of long yellow flannel drawers belonging to 1909, with a deep cotton waistband, cotton buttons and the usual centre front and back opening, extending to the waistband. They are very prosaic indeed. The knee-band is also buttoned, and to judge by their size they must have extended almost to the calves of E. Roote, whose name-tab they carry.

Formidable bloomers, often looming large beneath knee-length skirts, were the Edwardian lady's main concession to the needs of sport and games. But in general she entered into her various pastimes in the full panoply of underwear, from corsets to petticoats, and for tennis she wore ankle-length dresses or skirts. There was no sports outfit, outer or inner; Mrs Pritchard found games mostly unpleasing, because of the unattractive items of attire they demanded. Tennis, played in flat shoes, could attract only the avid enthusiast, but it was, she noted thankfully, possible to bicycle in elegant high heels and in normal clothes. By this time improved machines had banished most of the knickerbockers worn by early women cyclists.

12

Towards a Straight Line
From 1908

Fashion never stays still, and the days of the mature, full-blown beauty in her flowing skirts and frothing, be-frilled and copiously shaped underwear were almost over by about 1907, never to return. The great change, and what was nothing less than the start of modern fashion, came when Paul Poiret, a rising young Paris couturier, introduced a slim, up-and-down fashion line, banishing at a stroke the curved 'S'-shaped figure and its accompanying *mêlée* of elaborate underwear. Instead, he brought into fashion a natural shape, something unheard of throughout history with the partial exception of the brief Directoire period of about a century before. The purpose was similar: 'It was', he said later in his autobiography *My First Fifty Years*, 'in the name of Liberty that I proclaimed the fall of the corset and the adoption of the brassière, which, since then, has won the day. Yes, I freed the bust, but I shackled the legs' – a reference to the 'hobble' skirt which was an outstanding but contradictory feature of his 'liberation', but which was soon modified.

The change was not as simple as that, and though Poiret was mainly responsible, it happened because women were ready for it, as all fashions do. Their way of life was moving into a new, wider dimension in work, play and public and private activities. The leisured, wealthy woman was ceasing to be the important woman and was therefore ceasing to be the leader of fashion. The busy, active, middle-class woman, occupied at work or in the home, was taking over.

Nor, in practical terms, did Poiret banish the corset. Most women continued to wear it for many years to come, though he is said to have forbidden his personal clients to wear it. He did, however, lead the way to the first corset that left the waist unrestricted, the hips and eventually the bust unexaggerated. He banished the accepted 'S'-shaped corset and with it went the unnatural 'kangaroo' stance, the exaggerated backward-flowing hips, the constricted waist and finally the main

124   A longer corset in 1909

elaborations of the projecting bust. For the first time the fashionable woman stood upright and stood free – or nearly so. The qualification was due to the fact that the vogue for a straight figure led to a corset which, though near-tubular and low in the bust, was so long that it went nearly down to the knees. It was in 1908 described by a fashion journal as being 'cut so deep that to sit down would appear an impossible feat'. This very long corset persisted for a number of years, while the narrow skirt was in fashion, and it was, of course, laced up the back and fastened in front with the busk fastening. It had heavy suspenders which were clipped to the stockings just above the knee.

The bust bodice continued to increase in popularity from this time, and at first there were no outstanding changes in its construction. The bust remained upholstered, with padding and boning built into bust bodices, bust pads added and breast-plates of stiffly starched cotton or lace frills pinned on to their fronts by flat-chested fashionable women. Changes were, however, imminent in the shape of the bust bodice.

The word 'brassière' is recorded by the Oxford Dictionary as having been introduced in 1912. It was, however, used prior to that date in America, where in 1907 an illustration in *Vogue* was captioned 'the brassière'. Why this word brassière was adopted is something of a mystery. Although French, it is obsolete there in the meaning of a bodice, and neither was nor is used in France in the sense given it to replace the earlier 'bust bodice'. In French a brassière is usually an infant's under-bodice. Larousse's famous dictionary cites various other meanings, including a harness and, in the plural, leading strings or the shoulder straps of a rucksack, but not our 'brassière'. In France this garment is known as a *soutien-gorge*. The origin of our word would seem to lie with someone with an imperfect knowledge of French; dare we blame America for inventing the name? The now prevalent diminutive, 'bra', does not appear to have been used before about 1937.

125 Boned bust bodice in white cotton, *c.*1913

America was responsible for a major innovation in brassière design when, in 1913, Mary Phelps Jacob (later better known as Caresse Crosby) invented a new kind of brassière that was soft, short and so designed that it gave clear natural separation between the breasts. Then a fashionable New York débutante, she was in revolt against the whalebone bodices and corsets of the time and she contrived her bra with the help of her French maid, using two handkerchiefs and baby ribbon. Later she was persuaded to make copies of it for friends and then she planned to exploit it. She called it the Backless Bra and in November 1914 she was granted a patent for it and planned to market it, but was unsuccessful in doing so. She lost interest, but later, after her marriage to the first of her three millionaire husbands, she sold the patent to Warner Bros. Subsequently in her book *The Passionate Years* she claimed of 'the brassière' that 'I did invent it'. In fact she invented one design, but the garment had been in existence by name for at least six years before her invention and in a great variety of shapes since the last decade of the nineteenth century. It had, however, always been long, coming over the corset, and it was boned and rigid. Caresse Crosby introduced the modern concept of a brief style which was free of bones and left the midriff free. In that respect her design was revolutionary and pioneered future trends that would begin to show themselves in the 1920s. She lived to see innumerable developments in the bra, and died early in 1970.

126 Caresse Crosby's 1914 brassière

The 'hobble' skirt in its extreme form had only a limited appeal, being wearable only by the leisured and therefore a last concession to their claim to be exclusive leaders of fashion. But, modified by slits and hidden pleats, the new straight skirts which became fashionable from about 1908 meant that the swirl and sway of many petticoats, the pride and glory of Edwardian dress, disappeared. The petticoat changed completely and became a slim tube of fine silk or cotton which added no bulk to the sought-after slim silhouette. To wear more than one would be unthinkable. It could be full-length from shoulder to hem, or waist-length, as had been usual in Edwardian fashion, but in both cases there were no more of the gathered flounces which had called for five or

127   Corsets move towards the new clinging line in 1909

six yards of broderie anglaise, lace or frills. The full-length style, the Princess petticoat, also became known as the slip. The pretty camisole, sometimes called a slip-bodice, was added to or replaced the bust bodice for many women as the straight figure became general and the bust less accentuated.

With some resemblance of the new line to that of the Directoire period, slim-fitting knickers, closed in style, came into fashion and were called Directoire knickers. They were worn for many years and, though no longer a fashion, continued to be worn almost to our own time. They were similar to bloomers, but narrower, with elastic at knees and waist. The open style of knickers continued to co-exist with

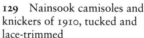

129 Nainsook camisoles and
knickers of 1910, tucked and
lace-trimmed

130 Combination petticoat of
1910, elaborately tucked and
decorated with lace

closed styles until the First World War, when closed styles became
general.

A foretaste of changes to come in underwear was the 'skirt knicker'
or 'divided skirt', first worn about 1906–1908. This was wide-skirted,
like contemporary open knickers, but was an abbreviated skirt,
buttoned between the legs. It foreshadowed both the later wide French
knickers and the cami-knickers of the 1920s and 1930s.

The chemise became narrower and shorter, in key with fashion, but
was gradually ousted by the slimmer vest or undervest, of wool, silk or
cotton. Combinations were increasingly worn because they reduced
the bulk of the underwear. They were worn universally by men,
women and children, and varied from porridge-coloured Jaeger styles
to the finest silk, as is seen from many store catalogues of the time
which still survive.

A new relaxation in dress came about 1908 when the high, boned
neckline which had been a feature of the Edwardian lady's day dress
began to give way to round necklines, either plain or finished with a
narrow frill. Poiret claimed credit for this liberation, and so did Lucile,
his sworn enemy, who dated it to the years immediately before 1914
and also said she was the originator of the Peter Pan collar. Both,
however, appeared in store catalogues by 1910. A further concession to
comfort was the 'V' neck, which appeared about the same time.

Though very moderate, it was condemned on grounds of both health and morality. Modesty vests came in to modify the revelation of the bare throat. Small squares of fine lawn, silk or georgette, often trimmed with embroidery or lace, they were pinned on to the other underwear with tiny brass pins or were attached by hooks or fasteners to the dress. They soon disappeared except among the elderly as the bare neck became accepted and was even given the frivolous name of the 'glad' neck – the first 'fun' name applied to a way of dress, to be followed by a series of similar descriptions for various undergarments.

The relaxation in women's underwear was echoed at this time in that of young girls. Through most of history until the later nineteenth century even very small girls were dressed as miniature grown-ups. Constricting corsets and tight lacing, as has already been recorded, were advocated for even the pre-teens in the crinoline era. But from about 1880 there was a gradual change and young people began to have their own kind of clothes.

A stayband had traditionally been worn from infancy by both sexes, for warmth as well as support, though it was usually dropped after babyhood in the case of boys. It took many forms and was made in depths varying from 3 inches to 14 inches. The most usual style was a flat, unshaped stiff band made of red or grey cloth on the outside, with an interlining of hessian and a white lining. The band was usually corded, for firmness, and the more luxurious ones were quilted with a layer of wadding between the outside and the lining. There were cut-out underarms and tape straps going over the shoulders. These bands were either buttoned in front or fastened there with a large hook and eye.

From the age of about ten girls wore a more shaped type of bodice, but one of similar construction, corded or boned. A modified version of this continued to be worn during the first quarter of the present century, but its popularity was waning. The big breakaway came in the appropriately named Liberty bodice, introduced by the corset firm of Symington in 1908. A soft knitted garment, with nothing more formidable than bands of tape to keep it in shape, it was quite simply a front-buttoning bodice. In a few years it became world-famous, ousting the old restricting staybands and bodices, and the output of it rose steadily year by year to an annual 3,500,000. In 1923 a light-weight version, the 'Peter Pan' fleecy bodice, was added, and was also very successful.

The Liberty bodice was part and parcel of the normal young girl's underwear for nearly half a century, and many middle-aged and elderly women of today can recall wearing it. It is still manufactured and it continued to be quite widely worn until the late '50s, when manufacturers began to cater for the teenager's increasingly sophisti-

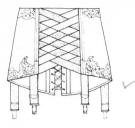

131 The dancing corset, c.1914, short, light and prettily trimmed, came in with the tango

132 Lawn combinations of 1913

133 Fine white lawn open knickers with embroidered net and lace insertion, 1912

cated tastes by designing young ranges of bras, suspender belts and, more recently, pantie-girdles, all specially styled for the adolescent, growing figure.

The waistline continued to be easy and natural in the years up to 1914, with even a tendency to bypass it in a revival of high, Empire lines about 1909. This meant that corsets became shorter and less heavily boned, and this was encouraged by a factor quite outside underwear fashion's own dictates. The tango came into vogue in America in the spring of 1911 and in a year or two was the rage everywhere, among old and young. Its vogue continued during and after the First World War. Its violent, jerky contortions and the heady excitement of its South American rhythms meant that freedom of movement was all-important and it probably had more than fashion to do with the diminishing size and severity of corsets at this time. It was followed, before the First World War, by even more hectic American dances, among them the Turkey Trot and the Bunny Hug, and in 1912 Ragtime came across the Atlantic, with the revue *Hullo Ragtime* opening at the London Hippodrome in December 1912. Mr and Mrs Vernon Castle, the famous dancers, made their appearance in the entertainment world before 1914, she with her bobbed hair, lithe, boyish figure and slim dresses, a blue-print of the girl of the 1920s.

Slinky, sheath-like dresses by Poiret, worn with next to nothing underneath and corsetless if he had his way, were the fashion that went with all this – before 1914. Fashionable corsets, by 1914, included narrow, almost boneless belts, with sections of criss-cross ribbon. In 1914 an advertisement in the *Sketch* of 12 April, proclaimed: 'The revolution in woman's dress demands also a revolution in corsetting her. Freedom is the dominant note in all that relates to modern woman, and it is this freedom which Marshall & Snelgrove have so successfully achieved in their new style of corsetting, without any loss of graceful symmetry'.

During these pre-war years underwear was continuing to become more modern in materials and conception, though many designs still remained traditional. Thus a pair of 1913 combinations, now in the Victoria and Albert Museum Collection, is made of gossamer-fine white lawn, trimmed with a mass of very delicate lace at bust and legs. There are pink satin ribbon shoulder straps, foreshadowing a future almost universal feature of underwear, and pink satin ribbon is slotted round the bust and waist. There is much elaboration of lace at the legs, the outside edges of which are slightly cut up to allow further lace trimming. But this garment is still open between the legs back and front, the join occurring only at the waist and knees. A pair of knickers, dated 1912, has the same characteristics of being made of material fine enough in texture to please the most modern taste, lavishly frilled with

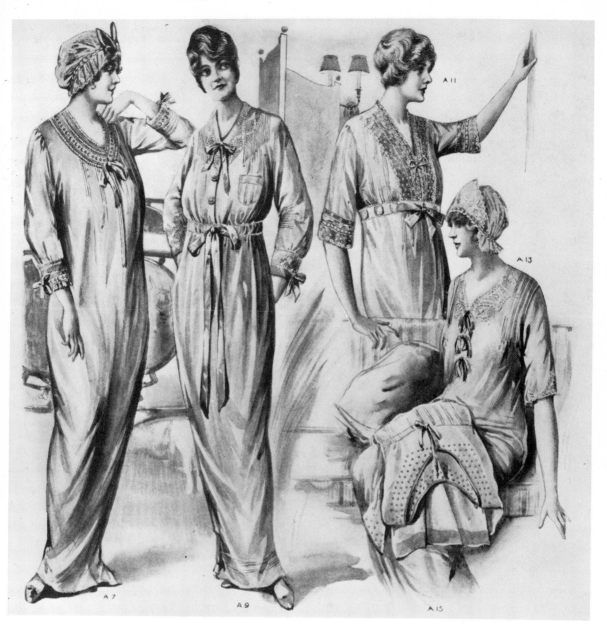

lace, plus lace insertion, tucks and embroidery. They are darted on to a narrow waistband and are buttoned down the sides, but they too remain open nearly to the waist.

The chief fashion innovation of the immediate pre-war years was the tunic. A short, full skirt began to be worn over the 'hobble' which had become so widely adopted that it was no longer pleasing to fashion leaders. Tunics of great variety, including wired 'lamp-shade' ones, gave scope for enterprise and novelty.

134 Nightdresses of 1914 shared the vogue for lace trimmings

13

World War One, then the 'Twenties and the boyish figure 1914–1929

The First World War did not bring any significant or immediate changes to fashion, because at the outset civilian life was not greatly affected and the delusion that peace would return in a few months was widespread. Women's organisations, despite their urgent efforts to be allowed to do some useful service, were pushed aside and women were expected by the ruling male chauvinists to be content to be the comfort and solace of tired warriors. Thus fashions, both under and outer, as seen in photographs and store catalogues and in costume collections, show largely a continuation of the styles of the pre-war years. There was even an increase of femininity in lace-trimmed lingerie, tea gowns and evening dress.

When, in 1915, the urgent need for women to play a part in the war effort was realised by the authorities, it might have seemed natural that a revolution would take place in their dress, as in their lives. In Britain the Women's Service Bureau recruited one and a half million women for civilian jobs, where they replaced men. In addition to pouring into munition and other factories women became civil servants (162,000 of them went into the new ministries set up in Whitehall), house painters, electricians, van drivers, bus conductors, porters and 'signalmen' on the railways. In 1917 they were introduced into the Police force, and early in that year the first regular women's service corps, the Women's Army Auxiliary Corps, was formed, to be quickly followed by the Women's Royal Naval Service and the Women's Royal Air Force Service. In these and supplementary services 150,000 women were enrolled.

The women who went into uniforms wore strictly utilitarian underwear but this had little to do with fashion, which remained static and continued to have its pre-war look, especially where underwear was concerned. Under the pressure of anxieties and tragedies and growing scarcities of everyday commodities there was neither time nor in-

135   Combinations of 1916 in finest cotton, trimmed with ribbon-slotted lace insertion and frills

clination for new fashions, even among women not actively engaged in war work of some kind.

One change, however, there was, of a practical kind. About 1915 the narrow skirts which were still fashionable disappeared. Very full ones replaced them. The logic of this was that wide tunics were by this time often worn over tube skirts. By abolishing the tube and lowering the tunic an above-ankle skirt, wide enough for service uniforms and for the many strenuous activities now being undertaken by women, was created without wholly discarding accepted fashion. This meant fuller petticoats, a temporary abandonment of a slim line and therefore further freedom in corsetry.

The main footnote to fashion history contributed by the First World War was a fashion that never was. This was an attempt in 1918 to introduce into Britain a National Standard Dress for women – a garment without hooks or eyes or metal buckles, which was designed to be an 'outdoor gown, house gown, rest gown, tea gown, dinner gown, evening dress and nightgown'. The mind boggles. It was the first and last attempt of the kind.

There was, however, some progress made on the wearing of brassières during the war. Whether this was partly due to the realisation that the support of this garment contributes both to health and comfort (as was to be promulgated later), it is difficult to say. Probably at that time brassière designing had not got far in this direction. The main need for a brassière was that the softer fashion lines of the immediate pre-war years were maintained in clothing. In 1915 it was said that 'a pretty bust bodice or a brassière counts quite as much an essential as a corset'. 'Gowns of utmost softness and semi-transparency have made a bust support essential', advised a fashion magazine in 1916. Evening dresses were of this type and so was the less formal and increasingly popular house dress, precursor of the later cocktail dress. In what seems a parody of a wartime rallying, all-together call, another fashion publication, *The Lady*, in the same year declared of brassières: 'The French and American women all wear them and so must we'. Friends and allies, stand together!

In general, however, the First World War left fashion untouched, even uniforms retaining the ankle-length skirts and bulky jackets of civilian styles. Though British casualties were heavier than in any other war in history, the rationing schemes imposed upon the civilian community were limited to food and did not, as in the Second World War, extend to clothing or lay down regulations upon what could be worn and how it could be made. The result of this was that post-war dress and underwear showed little immediate evidence of what, in retrospect, is regarded as a major watershed in history, the end of a long era, the first step into the unknown.

The fashions of the 1920s have been much dramatised and a stereo-type of a knee-length tube and a pudding basin hat under which figure and hair are respectively crushed out of existence has become accepted as the blue-print of a decade. In fact, however, things were very different. The wartime full, above-ankle skirts prevailed in 1918 and 1919. By 1920 skirts became somewhat shorter and narrower. They fell to the ankles in 1923, started rising again in 1924 and until 1927 were calf-length and, to a limited extent among the young and fashion-able, just below the knee. They then began to drop again and remained round the calves through the 1930s. The extreme 'Twenties' look, so much decried, was therefore a matter of only some three years. The fashion writers, perhaps in a post-war enthusiasm, exaggerated. For

THE SWEET ENCHANTMENTS OF CREPE DE CHINE

L.O. 38. Jumper Pyjamas. A well-cut model, in good quality crepe de chine. pink, sky, heliotrope, white, and black 69/-

L.O. 48. Dainty Nightdress. Good quality crepe de chine, with attractive front formed of tucked ninon, in contrasting colour. Pink, sky, heliotrope, white, and black 69/-

Boudoir Cap to match 10/9

L.O. 33. Sleeve Camisole. In good crepe de chine, daintily trimmed lace and embroidered in contrasting colours. Pink, sky, heliotrope, and cream, 14/9

L.O. 41. Beautiful Nightdress. Made in heavy British crepe, embroidered in dainty colours. Sky, pink, heliotrope, and white 45/9

Boudoir Cap 12/9

L.O. 42. Chemise, to match 19/6

L.O. 43. Knickers, to match 19.6

L.O. 44. Combinations, to match 29/6

HARRODS LTD   26   LONDON SW 1

136 Lingerie, nightdresses and pyjamas of 1919 follow pre-war lines and are still very elaborate. By Harrods

most women, the fashions of the 1920s were wearable, comfortable, becoming and in many respects more like those of the later 1970s than any others since then.

Nor did change, when it came, come quickly. Underwear shows this clearly. Cami-knickers of 1920 at the Victoria and Albert Museum, which present closed and open styles simultaneously, continue in the pre-war tradition of fussy prettiness. An English pair of cami-knickers (the name had become usual about 1916) are richly decorated with lace, have ribbon shoulder straps, but are open from the waist. Of the same year are a French pair, again with lots of lace, both as edging and as inserts, fine pleats, pink satin shoulder straps – but these are in the closed newer style, with a very big gusset. Closed directoire knickers, dated 1919, are in the same collection. They are of fine silk in violet and black stripes, with elastic at the waist and at the legs, which are finished with a frill and a bow at the outside. What mainly dates them is that, like all underwear of the time, they are so astonishingly big.

That, however, was soon to change, like other things. Women had emerged from the war with a new outlook. They had been given responsibility and had proved themselves worthy of it. The immediate effect in Britain was the giving of the parliamentary vote to all women

138 Closed cami-knickers in cream silk with fine pleating and wide bands of lace insertion strike a new note in 1920

over 30 in the Representation of the People Act which, after a long course of several months in both Houses of Parliament, finally received the Royal Assent on 6 February 1919. In 1928 the franchise was extended to women on the same terms as men, at the age of 21, and the much-talked-of (but inaccurate) 'Flapper Vote' came into existence.

In the first flush of emancipation and the 'equality' with men, signified by the vote and the increasing part the working girl and the career woman were playing in the post-war community, it was natural, if impulsive and rather unconsidered, for women to rush to demonstrate their equality with men by suppressing physical differences. There was a strong move of fashion to flatten the bosom, narrow the hips and bypass the waist. Fashion, which for hundreds of years had lived by exaggerating in turn the main female physical characteristics, now set about eliminating such features. The ideal figure was a straight line. The natural waist was almost non-existent, but belts and sashes were worn somewhere round the hips. The brassière assumed a form as unlike the Edwardian and pre-war bust bodice as could be imagined and was different from anything previously contrived. It became a

139   The straight line of the 1920s seen in 'underskirts' of 1920 in a Harrods' catalogue

flattener pure and simple. An essential part of the straight look, it was a single, slightly side-darted but otherwise straight band, usually of strong cotton or firm broché. It ran round the body from under the shoulders to the waist, with shoulder straps to support it. Its aim was to combine with a perfectly straight corset to produce a cylinder from chest to hips, regardless of natural contours and anatomy. It was the 'boyish' look, the first fashion essentially devised for the young and slim, though followed by all to some degree.

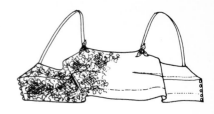

Nearly every corset manufacturer now came into the brassière market. One famous style was presented in 1922 with the claim that it was the only one to 'give the wearer a perfectly flat form from the shoulder to hem . . . and does not push up the bust'. Many of these brassières still exist in the collections maintained by certain corset companies, notably Symingtons of Market Harborough. In materials like heavy broché, usually pink, they were made with little change of style for many years. Some had side fastenings and others had all-elastic backs and no fastening, so must have been drawn over the head.

What effect had this flat figure on the corset? For the slim it meant real freedom and sometimes the girl of the 1920s anticipated her grand-daughter of half a century later by abandoning the corset. Instead she wore a narrow suspender belt, to keep up her stockings. Alternatively she wore a light unrestricting foundation garment and she again anticipated the future by discarding the name 'corset', due for future opprobrium, and calling it a belt or girdle. The escape from the past had to be complete. Elastic was beginning to be used to a considerable extent in corsetry at this time, as will be explained later, and shop catalogues of the early 1920s refer to 'corsets of woven porous elastic' (1923) and to wrap-round rubber corsets (1925).

For those whose natural curves defied fashion's dictates, firm corsets were, however, very necessary. Various wrap-round styles with front busks were worn, usually low on the hips and rising only slightly above the waist. In spite of the development of new, lighter corset materials from this time, this type of corset, rigid and heavily boned, usually still back-lacing, continued to be made for nearly half a century as a profitable, if decreasing, section of the corset trade. Older women, used to this kind of 'armour', found it difficult to discard in favour of the lighter but equally functional garments available in more up-to-date materials.

As the aim of the corset and brassière now was to provide an un-broken line down the whole torso, it was a logical conclusion that a one-piece garment would soon be evolved with this in view. What was at first known as the corselette appeared in America in 1919 and in Britain a year or two later. 'After years of separation', stated a US corset trade publication's retrospective survey, 'with high and low-bust

142   Corselette in mercerised
cotton with side panels of
knitted elastic, *c.*1925

143   Broché corselette with
elastic side panels, 1928

corsets, the fully confining brassière and the corset became integrated
in one completely supporting garment. It was laced, boned and
gusseted within an inch of the wearer's life, but it was the first modern
foundation'. It soon became softer and easier. There were also long
brassières, with suspenders attached, for flapper trend-setters who
wanted to throw away their corsets along with their inherited in-
hibitions. Surprisingly there were no protests against the flattening of
the figure on health grounds, though the constricting brassières should
have raised an outcry.

The new tubular line of fashion offered no compromise with underwear that had always been identified with the exploitation of feminine
curves. As a result the '20s was a period of continual change. Underwear, in addition to becoming much less bulky and complicated, was
peeled down and far fewer garments were worn. The chemise was
narrow and brief and the newer vest was soon to oust it completely –
and to be in its turn relegated to winter only. Knickers became shorter
and less full. The waist petticoat was narrow and straight, as was the
Princess petticoat, renamed the Princess slip and then simply the slip.
It too became much simpler – usually a straight length of material with
ribbon shoulder straps.

A feature of the '20s was the number of combined undergarments
which appeared. Already there was the cami-knicker, introduced
during the war, about 1916, but enjoying its heyday in the '20s and '30s.

More ephemeral, but newsworthy at the time, were various complicated multiple undergarments. In 1923, when skirts were near ankle-
length and the silhouette was soft, clinging and rather drooping,
Debenham & Freebody disclosed 'the secret of slenderness' in a group
of composite undergarments that offered various permutations of what
would normally be separate items. Pride of place went to the 'Corslo'
silhouette, 'bust bodice, hip belt, jupon and pantaloon combined, top
part of best quality double satin, buttoned at the back, and boned with
two steels in front to support the figure, the two pairs of suspenders
attached to the garment are hidden by the knickers; the skirt and
knickers of heavy laundry pleated crêpe de Chine. Measurements
required when ordering: bust, waist and hips'.

The illustration shows a long flat bra, with shoulder straps, a belt
and an accordion-pleated ankle-length petticoat. A smaller drawing
reveals how the stockings were attached by concealed suspenders
under concealed knickers. It was the start of co-ordinates, but it seems
quite unnecessarily complicated.

There was also the new 'Corslo-Pantaloon'. When you put it on,
according to one persuasive advertisement, 'you have thus instantly
put on the equivalent of chemise, knickers, corset and camisole and
have secured the naturally supple and straight slender figure effect
which is absolutely demanded by the new fashion'. It was made in
cotton tricot, crêpe de Chine, ajoure and silk tricot, at various prices.

In addition, the new 'Corslo' was a recognisable corselette, but soft
and easy to wear, in contrast to the original grim American version of
1919. It is advocated as a garment suitable for wear with 'the most
fashionable day and evening gowns and dance dresses, while, as
absolute freedom for every movement is essential to the success and
enjoyment of tennis and golf, etc, it is a necessity and boon to the
sportswoman'.

Very high prices, in comparison to those of today, are a feature of the
good quality underwear of the years between the wars. Matching sets
of nightdress and underwear are usual, and some reason for their
costliness may be that good quality garments were still all hand-made.
It is surprising and rather daunting to recall that this hand workman-
ship was a general feature of such underwear not only then but also up
to the Second World War. Notable too is the range of colours offered
in store catalogues in the '20s. It is far wider than would normally be
obtainable today and comprises, for typical garments, pink, sky,
mauve, yellow, peach, coral, ivory, champagne, saxe, vieux rose,
cyclamen, apple green, jade and black.

Other similar underwear is made in pure silk milanese, also at high
prices and in a choice of from six to ten colours. Combinations are
made in lace wool, as are chemises and knickers. Cashmere and silk

144   Combined bust bodice and hip confiner in broché with lace top, 1925

combinations were also worn by the fashionable woman of this time and were made in pink and white, but the chemises and knickers also came in sky, mauve and lemon.

As early as 1925 there is a brassière with a suggestion of natural curves. It has an adjustable centre front strap which breaks the flat bandeau front and suggests the coming introduction of bust cups because for the first time it separates the two breasts. An unusual garment of this time, illustrated in store catalogues, looks like an early corselette but is described as 'for use as a brassière and corset cover to disguise the line of the corset and give a perfectly smooth effect. It can also be used for bathing' – presumably under the swim-suit. It comes in white or black mesh materials in two qualities and a large range of sizes. It seems to have been a success, because it appears again in 1927 and 1928, by which time it is made in artificial silk – a new arrival.

Catalogues also show a 'combined bust bodice and hip confiner', with a lace top and the promise of firm control over the hips. It is made in two qualities of pink broché with lace top, and also in black. A hip girdle has elastic side sections and 'good diaphragm control'. It is a low corset, starting at the waist, straight and firm-looking, and made in various styles. Very similar is a well-designed 'topless corset' (a prophecy of the '60s and Rudi Gernreich) in broché, but something with a difference is a 'rubber reducing girdle with front or back lacing and lightly boned'. In pink covered rubber, it is made for tall or short figures.

Other lingerie of 1925, recorded in catalogues, consists mainly of matching sets of nightdress, chemise and knickers in satin or crêpe de Chine, but there are now more cami-knickers than in 1923. They include 'new shape step-in' cami-knickers and two other pretty designs, described as 'exact copy of French model'. Princess petticoats hang straight from shoulder straps and have, naturally, become shorter.

There are other garments in fine lawn, including hand-made linen lawn cami-knickers and an embroidered pair, with fine pleated side panels, in French lawn – again hand-made. Milanese silk is another favourite fabric for vests and matching 'skirt knickers'. Waist petticoats, slim and narrow, are numerous and include a sports petticoat in crêpe de Chine, with slits at the sides; one in pleated shantung, another in 'super milanese'; a yoked one in printed crêpe de Chine and a 'dainty' one in 'the best quality crêpe de Chine, exquisitely hand-embroidered in Richelieu work' – which can be made to order in three days in any colour desired!

The hint of curves was, however, gaining strength. In 1926 it is stated that 'the bust was emphasised and the waistline indicated'. Women were becoming women again. In 1926–1927 came the real start of the shaped bust cup that was to be the main justification of the

145   Topless corset worn with milanese silk vest, 1925

existence of the brassière in succeeding years. Mrs Rosalind Klin, Polish-born director of the Kestos company, was unable to find a brassière that suited her taste and her interpretation of fashion's trends. She therefore started experimenting and, oddly enough, began exactly as had Caresse Crosby in 1913, with two handkerchiefs. She folded these crosswise and joined them into one piece with an overlap in front. Shoulder straps were sewn on to the top point at each side of the bust and on to the end of the 'hypotenuse' of both triangles. Elastic was attached there, and, after being crossed at the back, was

146 (*above left*) Step-in cami-knickers in crêpe de Chine, 1925

147 (*above right*) Crêpe de Chine cami-knickers with elastic at knee, 1927

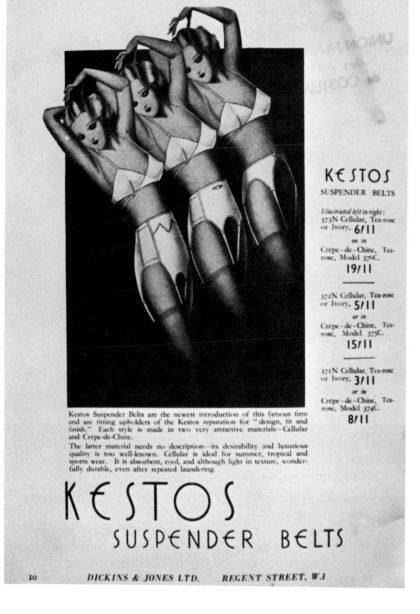

KESTOS
SUSPENDER BELTS

Illustrated left to right:
373N Cellular, Tea-rose
or Ivory, **6/11**
or in
Crêpe-de-Chine, Tea-
rose, Model 376C.
19/11

372N Cellular, Tea-rose
or Ivory, **5/11**
or in
Crêpe-de-Chine, Tea-
rose, Model 375C.
15/11

371N Cellular, Tea-rose
or Ivory, **3/11**
or in
Crêpe-de-Chine, Tea-
rose, Model 374C.
8/11

Kestos Suspender Belts are the newest introduction of this famous firm and are fitting upholders of the Kestos reputation for "design, fit and finish." Each style is made in two very attractive materials—Cellular and Crêpe-de-Chine.

The latter material needs no description—its desirability and luxurious quality is too well-known. Cellular is ideal for summer, tropical and sports wear. It is absorbent, cool, and although light in texture, wonderfully durable, even after repeated laundering.

KESTOS
SUSPENDER BELTS

10   *DICKINS & JONES LTD.   REGENT STREET, W.1*

148 The original Kestos bra, with the newly fashionable suspender belts of the late 1920s and 1930s

149   Knickers in crêpe de Chine with all-over flounces of lace, worn with matching chemise, 1927

buttoned to the brassière under each 'cup', which was darted under the bust to give it more shape. This style became almost the synonym for the brassière for many years. You didn't buy a brassière, you bought a 'Kestos'. Other variations followed, and the shape is very similar to that of the 'no-bra' of 1965 and of many of the very natural-shaped bras of 1969 and 1970.

Once shaping and separation had been achieved, further developments in the brassière were to be expected. Deeper bust cups were achieved in 1928 by a disc-like construction of the two sides. Circular stitching, so popular in the 1950s, was also first introduced as a way of giving a rounded shape about 1928.

The new idea of the brassière as a controlling garment, and not a flattener (as in the early 1920s) or a bust-maker (as in the later nineteenth and early twentieth centuries) caught on quickly. In 1927 advertisements showed an 'uplift bodice in good quality silk tricot'. It was a bandeau bra with two rounded cups. Another style was 'a one-piece garment of elastic and tricot, designed for a figure requiring an elastic hip belt, with some bust control above waist. Made in cotton or silk elastic'. 'Control' is mentioned in descriptions of all the other corsets featured in that year, except for a hookside belt for dance or sports wear, in 'pink material'.

Princess petticoats, at fashion's dictate, were now knee-length, like outer fashions, and were almost indistinguishable from cami-knickers. Another of the combined garments favoured at this time was a petticoat with directoire knickers attached, made in crêpe de Chine, trimmed with écru lace. There were also cami-shorts – the shorts buttoning up the sides but otherwise 'little boy' style. Some designs were very fanciful. Knickers had rows upon rows of narrow lace on the legs; they were covered entirely with lace flouncing; they had deep fitted bands at the knee. And, like the other underwear, they were 'in all colours'.

An innovation, which was to herald a revolution in underwear fabrics, was mentioned quite unobtrusively in a 1927 catalogue. It appeared in the description of a 'locknit artificial silk unladderable Princess, excellent for wear', made in the usual wealth of colours. Cami-knickers in artificial silk milanese were another item, and there were vests, knickers and a 'cami-petticoat' in the same material.

The following year, 1928 saw little change in catalogued offerings of fashion, but cami-breeches, which look exactly like cami-bockers, are there. An unexpected item is a lace camisole 'suitable for evening wear'. This was the last stand of this garment, rarely worn by 1929. Locknit artificial silk, 'unladderable', again appears as a popular underwear fabric.

Corsetry showed some innovations. There was a deep brassière in

150   Deep brassière with artificial silk bust sections and attached suspenders, 1928

artificial silk, with 'firm control across the diaphragm' and, as was usual then, long suspenders to anchor it to the stockings. A very straight-line 'one-piece garment' – a corselette – in white broché was described as 'suitable for many types of figure'. An elastic pull-on belt in pink cotton elastic was a newcomer, heralding the great progress being made at this time in the manufacture of elastic for corsetry. There was also an uplift bodice, in net, a brief brassière with two distinct cups and a separating section in the front, meant for a small or medium figure and made in sizes 30–34. What we would call a long brassière was also described as a bodice 'to cover the top of a low corset'.

The nineteen-twenties, in addition to paring down feminine curves and establishing a 'girlish' style of dress, also modified many of the

151 Uplift brassière in net, with boneless girdle with elastic side panels, 1928

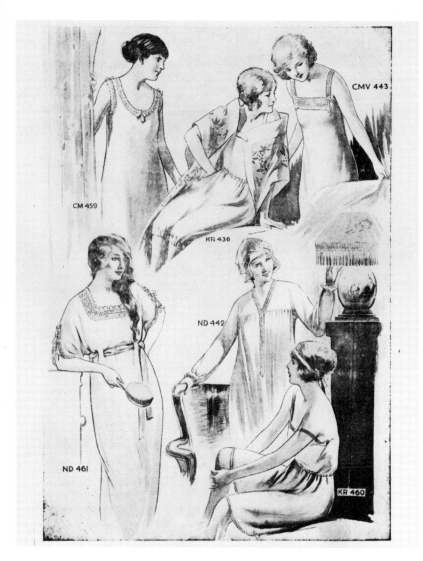

152 Nightdresses, even when of wool, become prettier in the 1920s

words hitherto used to describe underwear. Cami-knickers was, of course, from about 1916 used to describe a new garment, but underwear, from its elegant late Victorian and Edwardian description as 'lingerie', became collectively 'undies'. Petticoats were called colloquially 'petties' before they became 'slips'. Knickers were 'knicks', then in the '30s, 'pants' and 'panties' and finally, but not till the '50s, became 'briefs'. Combinations, on their way out, became 'combs' and the brassière after being called a 'BB', became the 'bra' about 1937.

Nightdresses shared in the increasing glamour and prettiness of underwear in the 1920s, and were often included in the matching sets which were advertised lavishly in store catalogues. Silk, lace, baby ribbon and embroidery all featured in them and they became part of the growing mass market for glamorous lingerie. Sleeveless nightdresses became fashionable; with them went matching jackets with sleeves and they became the favourite choice of the young. Pyjamas had been mentioned occasionally since the 1880s, but it took the First World War and its aftermath of young fashions to make them really popular as well as fashionable. They varied from tailored styles, similar to those of men, to pretty styles with wide trousers and feminine jumper tops. They were made in all materials, from cotton and gingham to silk and satin.

14

Material Changes in Corsetry and Underwear and their effect on fashion 1920–1939

By the late 1920s the centuries-long artificial shapemaking of women's figures had become a thing of the past and since then, for nearly fifty years, it has remained so, with one or two minor exceptions. These were mainly the built-up square shoulders of the years before, during and after the Second World War, and the exaggerated bosoms of the mid-'50s. Both of these differed from previous extravagances of underwear's fashion history in that they were entirely surface effects. The body beneath them remained natural and free of constriction or distortion, as it was before and after these artificial excrescences.

Corsetry, the obvious function of which is to improve on nature, for aesthetic or erotic reasons, was by this time doing so by means which usually respected nature. Increasingly, this purpose was based on understanding by corset companies and their designers of the anatomical structure of the body; of its bones, muscles and tissues and of the means by which foundation garments could not only follow nature but lend a helping hand when nature failed. Inevitably it must often do so, through imperfections in physique, weak muscles, excessive or insufficient weight and, despite all the care in the world, the inevitable ageing and therefore deterioration of the body.

There had in the past been no dearth of agitation about the damage done by wrongly fitted corsets, but there had been a lack of practical reformers and of ideas which could correct the evil without sacrificing accepted standards of elegance and abandoning fashion. In 1867, for instance, a doctor had proposed that the corset should be discarded and the crinoline suspended from the shoulders by braces so that constriction and weight could be taken away from the waist. A camisole, stiffened if need be, was also suggested as an alternative to the corset, with drawers and petticoats buttoned on to it. As this kind of underwear was inconceivable under the fashionable crinoline and, later, the bustle and long, tight bodice, a kind of anticipation of the 'sack' of the 1950s, had to be specified as outerwear. Needless to say, the fashion reform failed.

The first practical large-scale efforts towards liberating women's figures by a better kind of corsetry began when two American doctor brothers, Drs Lucien G. Warner and I. de Ver Warner, after serving in the Civil War, returned to New York to write books on women's diseases. In 1874 they began manufacturing a health corset and from their small beginnings grew the great company of Warner Bros, as famous in Britain as in the USA and notable as a pioneer of several future important innovations in foundationwear.

The return to nature in corsetry was, of course, part of the changing status of women. The whole history of underwear during the past forty or fifty years has reflected increasingly the social, psychological and economic effects of what must briefly be described by the rather out-worn word 'emancipation'. This meant that outerwear followed with increasing vigour and enterprise the trend towards freedom in the design and construction of clothes which had begun after the First World War. Outer clothes became less formal, underwear followed suit and that meant that, in practical terms, lightness, comfort and ease were sought in it. Class distinctions were breaking down. Spending power was being spread over a much larger section of the community. The masses expected their share in the good things of life. Everyone was making for the open-air. Sunbathing became popular and cover-up fashion died. Tennis stars wore knee-length or above-knee divided skirts by the late 1920s. Within the decade shorts were worn for cycling and sport and short skirts were accepted for skating.

These social changes showed themselves in simpler underwear and in the formulation of basics which were mostly established in the '20s and most of which have altered little in their general character during the years since then. They were and still are worn in very similar forms by people of all classes everywhere.

By about 1930 corset manufacturers began to feel that their products needed to pay much more attention to the great variety of women's shapes. The difference in measurements between bust, waist and hips varied very substantially from one woman to another but little atten-tion had hitherto been given to this either in outer or inner wear. Most garments were based on bust or waist measurement alone and sizing was usually worked out from casual measurements of limited numbers of women. Little wonder that so many women complained that 'their corsets were killing them'.

In America the corset firm of Gossard, which started there at the start of the present century, produced in its early days a chart defining 'nine perfect figure types', but at that time the subject was in an embryonic state in comparison with later studies. The first scientific

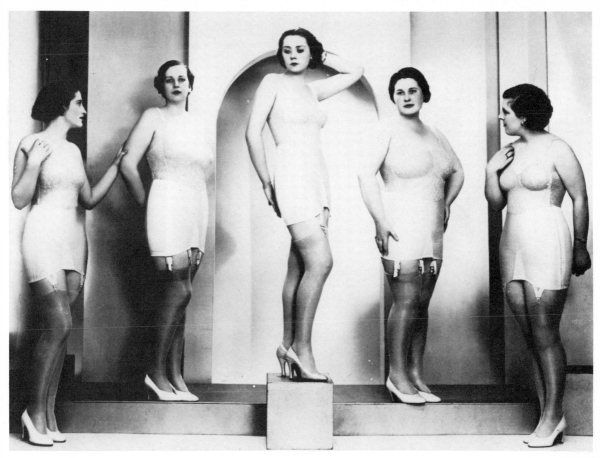

study of women's figures was an anthropometrical survey set on foot by Berlei, then operating in Australia, in 1926. With the co-operation of two professors of the University of Sydney and the Standards Association of Australia 26 measurements were made on every one of 5,000 women by skilled statistical staff, all endeavours being made to secure a representative sample of Australian women. The results were analysed and collated between 1926 and 1928 and showed that all women fell into one of five basic figure types, regardless of whether they were short or tall, fat or thin. This system was reviewed in depth by Berlei in Britain in 1976 and its validity was confirmed.

When in the 1930s natural curves became fashionable and comfort and ease were as much in demand as a good appearance, it became obvious that foundationwear needed to be made in a great number of styles and to a great number of measurements and permutations of measurements. When Berlei (UK) was established in 1930 it brought the system of sizing to Britain and applied it to a wide range of garments. It was evident that to acquire a properly fitting corset a woman had to be

153 Five figure types, a practical illustration, by models, of the Berlei system in the early 1930s

154 *(left)* A typical fashionable corselette of the 1930s

155 *(right)* 'Corsets must be fitted carefully', says an advertisement of the 1930s. The trained fitter was given much publicity

measured and fitted by a competent, trained saleswoman. For such training, leading corset manufacturers made themselves responsible, following certain variations of the figure type principle suited to different types of merchandise and ranging from as few as three to as many as seven such types. Though ideas about foundationwear have greatly changed since the 1930s, the qualified fitter still remains a vital link between the corset department and the customer in stores and speciality shops all over the country.

It is to the great credit of the foundationwear industry as pioneers of improved fashion technology that it was not until 1957 that the Board of Trade book *Women's Measurements and Sizes*, sponsored by the Joint Clothing Council, was published, with the claim to be 'the first scientific study undertaken in this country of body measurements of importance in the construction of women's garments', both outer and inner. It was based on a 1951 study in which about 5,000 women between the ages of 18 and 70 were measured, about 200,000 measurements being recorded. No further official study has been made; sadly, because it would be interesting to know if recent more liberated fashion attitudes, diet, weight-watching, increased activity and exercise, plus a quite different concept of corsetry and its partial abandonment, have affected those famous figure types and if so how? Has the proportion of women found in each category changed? Are there now fewer 'fatties'? What lies behind the fact that North Country women buy larger sizes of bras and corsets than those in the south? Why are Scotswomen more conservative in their tastes?

What has certainly changed is the sought-for ideal. Today's 'vital statistics' of 34–24–34 would please no age but our own. Meantime the average woman comes nowhere near them: she is 5 ft 3 ins tall, measures 37–27$\frac{3}{4}$–39 and weighs 9 st 7 lbs.

With the open air, sun-seeking cult, which began in the 1920s, the skin began to be exposed as never before by both sexes. Sleeveless, low-necked summer dresses exposed women's arms and an area round the throat and shoulders. Short skirts revealed legs and, though bare legs

156 Corsets made front-page advertisements, if not news, in 1930, when special corset weeks were held by stores all over the country

were not usual even on holidays until the start of the 1930s, it was in key with the new cult that stockings should be skin-coloured, in tones varying from a crude pink to a glaring sunburn but more usually a variety of beige and fawn shades. These began to replace black from about 1921 and have prevailed ever since. As they were so visible, pure silk was a coveted acquisition of the fashionable, but was at first expensive. For most people rayon was the everyday choice and, in comparison with later improvements, it was at first shiny, thick and clumsily shaped, consisting of a tube of knitting made on circular machines and failing to cling to the leg.

The fully fashioned stocking was at first mainly imported from America, Germany and other European countries. It was bought by the top end of the market. It was in April 1928, during the short-skirt era, that the Full-Fashioned Hosiery Company, one of the first in England to manufacture only fully fashioned stockings, was established with the aim of turning out 1,500 dozen pairs of silk and rayon fully fashioned stockings a week. It grew rapidly and by the early 1930s was producing sheer and service weight rayon and silk stockings of a good shape at a price that undersold the cheap German imports then dominating the market. By 1934 its pure silk stockings were being sold at 2/11 a pair. The woman of the 1930s had achieved elegance and the cult of the fully fashioned stocking was established, to last for some 30 years.

The main developments in underwear in general and to a special extent in foundationwear in the past half-century have, however, been due not only to fashion's changes but also, and much more, to something which had never happened before in the whole history of fashion – nor indeed in the history of mankind. This was a complete revolution in fabrics, consisting of the introduction of a multiplicity of new materials possessed of new properties. These, and the fibres from which they are made, are collectively described as man-made. This term is used generally to describe all fibres and fabrics other than those which have a natural origin, such as wool, cotton, silk and flax.

Man-made fibres are produced by the chemical treatment of certain raw materials, among the chief of which are wood pulp, cotton linters, petroleum extracts and by-products of coal. Such fibres and therefore fabrics are still being added to. They have scores of different names, properties and functions and the area of scientific development to which they belong covers the whole of plastics.

The conception of man-made fibres goes far back, although their general use belongs to our time. In 1664 Robert Hooke, an English scientist, suggested in his *Micrographia* that threads could be spun from an 'artificial glutinous composition', following the principle of the silkworm. In 1734 a French scientist, René A.F. de Réaumur, put forward the idea that gums or resins could be drawn out into fibres from which an artificial textile could be produced. But the first known patent for the manufacture of such a fabric was issued in 1855 to George Audemars, a Swiss chemist who had produced fibres from the inner bark of the mulberry and other trees. These he nitrated and dissolved in a mixture of ether and alcohol and then combined with a rubber solution to form a spinning mixture. Rayon, however, to which all this was leading, did not yet become a practical reality. The next step towards this end was taken by Sir Joseph Swan, an Englishman, who started by looking for a better carbon filament for electric light bulbs and in 1883 patented a process for making a filament by squeezing a nitro-cellulose solution into a coagulating medium and then denitrating the filament. He too failed to follow up the textile potentialities of this thread, though the cellulose acetate fibres he produced were crocheted up by his wife and shown at the London Inventions Exhibition of 1885.

The crucial step in developing rayon as a textile was taken about this time by Comte Hilaire de Chardonnet, often called 'the father of the rayon industry'. Beginning his experiments in 1878, he produced his first fibre in 1884 and exhibited articles made from it at the Paris Exposition of 1889. He obtained financial backing for a factory at Besançon in France, where the commercial production of acetate rayon started in 1891. Viscose rayon, which was to be the most successful kind, was the brain-child of three British chemists, Cross, Bevan and Beadle, who took out the first patent in 1892. It went into production in Britain in 1905 and in the USA in 1911, with the support of Samuel Courtauld. In 1911 Dr Dreyfus discovered and patented a method of producing acetate rayon which was developed by British Celanese, the company with which he was associated. It was, however, not until the early 1920s that rayon was of sufficiently good quality, attractive appearance and wearability to go into general use in the clothing and many other industries.

It happens that rayon and many of the man-made fibres subsequently developed have properties particularly suited to underwear. Here they superseded natural materials to a greater extent than in any other section of the clothing industry. The new rayon of the '20s very quickly found its way into underwear, and the main reason for this is conveyed by the name 'artificial silk' or 'art silk', which was first given to it. Now largely obsolete as a description and frowned upon by fabric manufacturers, who rightly credit rayon with new, improved qualities of its own, this description nevertheless explained the instant appeal of rayon in underwear. It brought the luxury look to the assertive new mass market. It made it possible for the ordinary woman of limited means to buy underwear which closely resembled the real silk and satin beyond her means. For the first time she could have pretty, attractively coloured underwear with a soft feel and a flattering cling that had up to that time belonged only to the luxury trade.

The new rayon underwear was by the mid-'20s being worn by women of all classes, although pure silk, crêpe de Chine and satin were to remain an appreciable part of the top end of the trade for nearly twenty years more.

In attractive pastel colours, lace-trimmed and embroidered, rayon opened up a new conception of underwear in general. It was to reign supreme for a generation. It was made in silk, satin, crêpe de Chine and other weaves. It also competed vigorously with the expensive knitted silk milanese which was popular in fashionable high-quality underwear. Knitted rayon, which was called locknit, dominated a large section of the mass market in inexpensive underwear for many years, during all the '30s and a considerable part of the '40s. It was the choice of the more down-to-earth section of the public, including a majority of older women. Locknit directoire knickers and slips with either built-up shoulders or straps were favoured by the more staid and practical women, while the younger and more fashion-conscious chose fine woven rayons for their French knickers and for lace-trimmed slips that varied comparatively little from those worn today.

Many of the garments made at this time were in fact not to change greatly for years. Some of them are still recognisably in general wear. They derived from the fashionable styles of the late '20s – French knickers, cami-knickers and Princess slips. All these garments became slimmer and altogether more fitting in style, with a younger look and shorter legs to the knickers and cami-knickers. Much of this slim underwear of the '30s was cut on the cross, both in the bust sections and in the skirt knicker parts of the garments, thus following the outerwear innovation made in Paris by Vionnet in the late 1920s. Diagonal seaming below the bust joined the two sections. *Vogue* in 1938 painted a grotesque picture of pre-bias-cut undies, comparing them to balloons and instancing cami-knickers as a garment in question. Nightdresses in particular acquired a new glamour and elegance by being bias-cut, with sinuous skirts flowing out to wide hems and exiguous clinging sleeveless tops. These were the high fashion ones, in beautiful silks and satins, lace-trimmed. More practical styles followed traditional lines and pyjamas varied from feminine jumper-top styles to plain tailored ones.

Knitted wool continued to be used for vests, as did cotton, and these were less bulky than in the past. Among young people they began to be worn only in winter or not at all. The brassière and girdle were considered by many people a sufficient first layer of underwear for warmer weather. Thus the corset or girdle and the brassière were worn next to the skin. Previously both had been worn over the vest or

157 Silk cami-knickers, cut on the cross, 1934

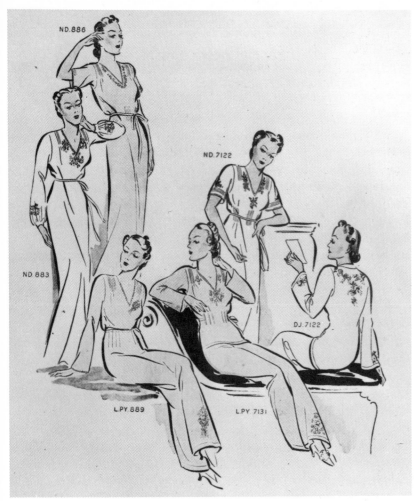

chemise. Combinations were relegated to the elderly and chemises remained past history.

Although fifteen years were to pass after the invention of rayon before a second and much greater invention in fabrics – that of nylon, also with special bearings on underwear and corsets, – was to be achieved, the '30s were the most momentous of all periods in history for corsetry. Within that decade the whole conception of it was changed. Materials, components and construction were all revolutionised, although the full fruits of the change were not to be seen until the post-war years, when still further developments in man-made fibres added new chapters to the story.

The big break-through for corsetry in the '30s did not, however, come so much from the man-made fibre developments as from a quite different source. This was elastic. Alone and unaided it created a new type of foundation which soon bore no resemblance whatever to the kind that had prevailed continuously, with variations in shape but not in basic construction or materials, for more than three and a half centuries. The new idea almost banished whalebone, steel, lacings, busks, heavy cottons and canvas. It made a clean break with the rigid, stiffened kind of corsetry that had been the only kind ever known.

Women of the 1930s were not ready to throw away their corsets, but they were ready for softer, more relaxed and comfortable fashions which required that they should throw away whalebone and busks, steel and stiffening. That they could do, thanks to elastic's opportune new developments. Shirts and sweaters, Chanel-type suits, the first slacks and shorts all followed a natural figure, far more closely and more revealingly than the first moves made in this direction by Paul Poiret and by the tube line of the 1920s. All fashions since then, however fantastic some of them have been and are, have been based on a 'natural' figure – which means one either uncorseted or wearing the new kind of supple, pliable foundationwear. Whether that is minimal in support or capable of firm control, the result is dependent almost entirely on elastic, natural or, more recently, man-made, and it had its beginnings and much of its development in rubber.

Unlike the man-made fibres which have been the main influence on other items of underwear in our time, rubber, which is the raw material of natural elastic, comes from a tree and is as old as the Malayan forests, and it was on rubber elastic that the corset revolution was based. The man-made counterparts, distinguished from the natural kind by being described first as elastomerics, and from 1976 in the EEC generic term as elastane, were not developed for practical corsetry purposes until the early 1960s.

In 1924 pieces of fossilised natural rubber, discovered in lignite deposits in Germany, were dated as belonging to the Eocene period, about 55 million years ago. Natives of Brazil have known of rubber for centuries and it was mentioned by Columbus. Although natural rubber originally came from various wild tropical trees and shrubs, from their roots, branches, leaves and fruit, for practical purposes the rubber tree is the only reliable commercial source. The rubber plantations of the Far East were started from seeds from the Amazon propagated at Kew in a series of experiments which began in 1873, but the large-scale development of the plantations belongs to this century.

The first big step that changed rubber from something used merely for rubbing-out was made by Thomas Hancock, who from 1820 to 1847 worked on the problem of elasticising rubber. He discovered a process of vulcanising it, mainly by the use of sulphur, and took out his first patent in 1820, with fifteen more to follow. This process gave rubber the 'snap back' that elastic means and, by making it resistant to heat and cold, rendered it a workable material. By the mid-nineteenth century this rubber was being used commercially for many purposes, from railway buffers to clothing.

It is an odd fact that although elastic has produced greater changes in corsetry than in any other section of clothing, corsetry was not the first to use it. Credit for this went to the men's footwear trade, which introduced elastic-sided boots in mid-Victorian times, while corsetry remained rigid until well into the present century.

An elastic knitted corset was mentioned in the official catalogue of the Great Exhibition at the Crystal Palace in 1851, but at this time 'elastic' was used in a different sense, to describe woven fabrics, and this cannot have been elastic in the modern meaning. The same catalogue also describes 'double silk elastic woven corsets, with the royal arms and national emblems inserted . . . woven to fit the body, and recommended for freedom of respiration'. One would like to have seen them.

The first factory for making elastic thread for the boot trade was set up by two brothers, W. & H. Bates, at Leicester in 1863. It widened its scope, but continued under that name until 1925, when it was taken over by the Dunlop Rubber Co. It became the biggest as well as the oldest in Europe and from it has stemmed a major part of important Anglo-American research into elastics, both natural and, more recently, mainly in the last decade, synthetic.

The concept of corsetry in the mid-nineteenth century and the limitations in manufacturing resources in the era of the crinoline and bustle made the association of ideas between elastic and corsetry very remote: so much so that the first recorded corset to be sold with elastic in it is dated 1911. It was called a sports corset – and the elastic was merely a three-inch band round the waist of a rigid garment.

During the First World War some elastic was used in wrap-round belts worn by women engaged in strenuous physical war work, which called for freedom as well as control in their corsetry. The first advertisement for a corset without lacing, but with elastic, appeared in the USA in 1913. In 1914 the 'dancing corset', with elastic in it, also appeared in the USA, then at the height of the tango craze.

Even in the '20s, however, the use of elastic in corsetry was very much limited by the fact that the only rubber obtainable was coarse and could be produced only in short lengths. Made on hand-knitting machines, this elastic could be fashioned and made in special shapes, but only to the very limited extent suitable for insets, gussets and waistbands in rigid garments. A wrap-round all-rubber corset, made of sheet rubber and called Madame X, appeared in the USA in 1923 but was short-lived. Similar garments were launched more successfully in the '30s, sometimes with the claim that they reduced the figure. The most successful and best-known rubber corset was the Charnaux of the

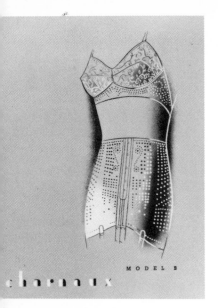

MODEL B

charnaux

159 The Charnaux girdle of the late 1930s was a big break-through for the figure-conscious woman of ample measurements

early 1930s, made with perforations and therefore more healthy and comfortable than some others. Sophisticated versions of the idea have been a feature of foundationwear from the '60s. One point about these rubber corsets is that for the first time it was advocated by the makers that they should be worn next to the skin. Previously corsets had been worn over vests or chemises, and sometimes even over petticoats. The difficulty in washing them was one practical reason for this, but as the corset became lighter and easy laundering became a strong selling point, it came to be worn next to the skin. The brassière had a similar history.

The difficulties regarding rubber elastic in corsetry centred upon the fact that the latex, as the milky sap of the rubber tree was called, coagulated quickly. It was therefore exported at first in hard 'biscuits', then, as the Far East plantations developed, in coagulated sheets. These were reconstituted in this country, being treated with chemicals to give them a 'kick' and then made into sheets about 100 yards long and 36 inches wide. Strips were cut from these and knitted up with rigid yarns for various purposes, including the first uses of elastic in corsetry. It was this shortness of length which limited the use of elastic during the '20s.

About 1930 came the big break-through that was to make elastic a basic material of all corsetry. A way was found of exporting the latex emulsion direct from the plantations. With certain processes of concentration and additives, such as ammonia, to prevent spontaneous coagulation, it was shipped in tankers which could carry 200,000 gallons of it, and was sent direct to the factories in sealed drums.

The importation of liquid latex revolutionised the manufacture of elastic thread. An entirely new process of extrusion was used. This process, developed by the Dunlop Rubber Company, meant that very fine elastic thread could be produced in immense lengths. The liquid latex, after going through various processes at the factory, was fed into machines at one end of which were rows of small glass capillary tubes. The mixture flowed through these into acetic acid baths, where it instantly coagulated in the form of continuous parallel rows of round threads. These could have a great variety of thicknesses which were controlled by the size of the nozzles and the rate of the flow. Various other processes followed, with the result that for the first time elastic threads, or Lastex, could be produced in the same lengths as and with similar degrees of fineness to other threads. Therefore these elastic fabrics could now be woven or knitted in substantial lengths and widths. The course of their development in this respect was subject to the process of adapting various kinds of machines to producing elasticised fabrics instead of the rigid ones to which they were accustomed.

The introduction of the new elasticised materials meant a new concept of corsetry. Figure control no longer depended upon boning, lacing and the imposition of a rigid kind of cage on the figure. Instead, support and control were created by means of the special tensions and 'pull' of the elastic in fabrics selected and used by the designer in such a way that they smoothed and moulded the figure gently. Health, comfort and appearance all benefited.

The most notable immediate result of the process of extruding rubber elastic was the introduction of the 'roll-on', the most famous corset of its time, with the additional distinction of having added a word to the English language, as well as a new item to the history of underwear. The first roll-on dates from 1932 in Britain and probably a year earlier in the USA. It replaced the hookside or busk-fastening corset for the younger and lighter figures – and for many more too, so great was its comfort. It dominated the 'light control' market for many years. If you belonged to that market you didn't talk of a corset any more; you said a 'roll-on' and got rid of what was already an unpopular word.

The roll-on was made on the circular knitting machine, which was already being used for elastic, so it was a 'natural' so far as innovations went. One of the main manufacturers of roll-on blanks (the actual 'tubes' without the suspenders) records that his company began to make them in 1932 and has been making them ever since, though with many improvements. The roll-on was also one of the first arrivals in the imminent new fabrics sphere of two-way stretch which Warner Bros are recorded as having introduced into corsetry in the USA in 1932. This was a direct result of the new fine, long elastic threads that were now available.

The '30s saw a continuous year-by-year development and variety in corset and brassière materials. These were of two kinds – elasticised and rigid. The latter consisted of a far greater variety of fabrics than we have today. One leading manufacturer, Berlei, who has kept catalogues and actual garments annually since 1931 used, during the '30s, grosgrain, four-fold voile, faille, satin, lace, broché, batiste, pekin net, milanese, crêpe de Chine, Breton net, Swami, satin brocade, piqué satin, plain and embroidered linen, voile, broderie anglaise, mercerised batiste, brocatelle and delustred satin. At the same time elastic materials were being developed. In 1934 Lastex batiste, hand-knitted elastic and chiffon Lastex yarn are mentioned. In 1935 it is said that 'all the best manufacturers now use Lastex', and nineteen are listed. It is described as 'the wonder yarn'. Among elasticised materials widely used were gripknit, French Lastex-yarn lace, satin Lastex, flowered satin power Lastex yarn, controlastic, aeroknit elastic panels and elastic net. In 1936 these were added to by power lace (lace with elastic power in it), and after a more or less similar picture for 1937, 1938 saw

160 The roll-on was the top favourite among young women of the 1930s

161 Backless corselette in figured batiste with bra top, *c*.1935

162   Light-weight Aertex girdle of 1938

163   Brassière in satin and lace, 1940

the use of Leno elastic and open-mesh elastic yarns. Woven elastics were added about 1939 and marked a big technical advance, but advantage could not be taken of the possibilities they opened up until after the Second World War.

During these pre-war years corsetry styles moved over steadily from busk-front and hookside wrap-ons to step-ins, semi-step-ins and corselettes. For younger and lighter women the roll-on was well to the fore. Laced-up garments were disappearing from ranges with any claim to fashion. Although in the early '30s moderate and, to a smaller extent, heavy boning persisted, it also was decreasing as elastics became more adaptable and versatile. Double material and stitching also often replaced bones as a means of firming garments. Figures were becoming more shapely, but with softer contours than in the past. In 1935 C.B. Cochran declared that his Young Ladies should have curves and the Young Ladies of the famous impresario of the '30s were the figure and fashion ideal of the time.

The '30s were years of backless evening dresses and many corselettes are described as being backless. By 1938 many were 'backless and boneless'. Stretch-down back panels became prominent in the later '30s. 1936 saw an all-elastic corselette with special two-way stretch panels both back and front. By 1939 most girdles were either step-ins or semi-step-ins, but the earlier hookside wrap-on styles persisted, and the traditional rigid corsetry, with its back-lacing, front busk and numerous bones, continued to be in production, though on a steadily diminishing scale. It is still not entirely dead. It is only within recent years that at least one major manufacturer closed down the 'rigid section', which a few others still maintain.

All through the '30s the predominant corset and brassière colours were pink or peach or variations on these tones, described as rose-beige, tea rose, apricot and other similar names. A very few garments were made in white, but other colours almost disappeared and black was very much in the luxury class.

An unexpected feature of corsetry of the '30s was the existence of garments at what even today would be a high price. In 1931 a corselette in peach satin and lace cost eight guineas – which in today's terms would be many times that amount. This was from the range of Berlei, a manufacturer who also sold garments priced in shillings. Among other items of the early '30s were corselettes, again in satin, in white, peach or pink, with lace and hand-knit elastic and a lace frill at the bottom, at six and a half guineas. In 1935 luxury was expressed in a 'de luxe semi-step-in controlette in black Lastex-yarn satin, specially lifted bust section in Alençon lace'. One step-in girdle in 1936 cost £5, and six guineas was the 1937 price of a 'de luxe' evening corselette in black satin with velvet appliqué on torso, modern uplift bustline and hand-knit elastic. Another surprising feature of old catalogues is the number of garments in the ranges. One company had 104 different brassières on its list in the mid-'30s, plus many dozens of belts and corselettes.

In review, the most remarkable thing about the underwear of the '30s was the extent to which it either created the styles and characteristics that still persist or else, particularly in foundationwear, anticipated developments generally associated with the post-war years, and especially with the '50s. Many of the innovations related to the brassière. This was described in the '30s as having cup busts, defined busts, uplift busts and even an accentuated bust-line. In 1935 in the USA Warner Bros introduced cup fittings for the first time. They had realised what now seems a very self-evident fact – that the measurement of the bust and the size of the breasts involve two different measurements, if the latter are to be accorded their 'natural' shape, and that the brassière must be designed to take both requirements into account. In this innovation there were four cup sizes, A B C and D, just as today. It was, however, some years before this system and the descriptions were generally adopted. Up to 1940 bust sizes alone were still being widely used in Britain, although descriptive sizes of bust cups were on record, in 1939, under the names junior, medium, full and full with wide waist.

The strapless bra was introduced in 1938, but although this anticipated its great success in the 1950s it did not succeed and it disappeared for many years. The wired bra, also due to take an important place from the '50s right up to the present, likewise made its first appearance in the immediate pre-war years. Examples of it are recorded in Britain in 1938, but it was not successfully established until the early '50s, when improvements in materials, techniques and design made it a highly favoured style. The first padded bra dated from the mid-'30s and inset foam pads were used by 1940.

The high bosom of post-war years appeared in 1939 bras and corselettes. The pointed bust and the exaggeration of the shape of the bust, also associated closely with the 1950s, originated in the Mae West era of the late '20s and '30s. Highly emphasised bust cups were created by means of circular stitching, another device familiar in the '50s, and also by stiffening inserted into the points of the cups. At both periods the emphasis on the bust was exploited by the film world. Bra-slips were also produced in the '30s. In 1932 in America Maidenform combined a brief bra with a slip to produce a 'costume slip'. This was the prototype of the bra-slip, which was to become an important part of the general range of underwear in the later '60s. Similar garments also appeared in Britain in the '30s. Spiral boning, an important innovation and amenity in corsetry and still part of contemporary foundationwear, first came into use in 1938.

Few inventions have contributed more to the comfort of corsetry than the zip fastener. The first steps towards it were made in America where, at the end of last century, Whitcombe L. Judson, a Chicago engineer, took out the first patent for a 'slide fastener'. The principle was right, but the actual appliance had a way of jamming or flying open without warning. A Swede, Dr Gideon Sundback, in 1913 produced the first marketable version by attaching the metal locks for the first time to

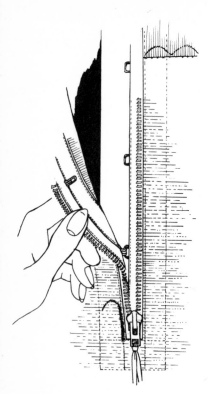

164 The zip fastener, a great boon to corsetry from the early 1930s

CHILPRUFE PURE WOOL

HOUSE GOWN 7243
Ample wrap over and heavily embroidered round hem. In Black, Almond, Duck-Egg, Ariel.

S.W. and Wms. 75 -
O.S. 4 6 extra.

H.G. 7247

HOUSE GOWN 7247. In Duck-Egg, Black, Ariel, Almond, Cornflower.

S.W. and Wms. 60 -
O.S. 4 6 extra.

H.G. 7243

Page 2

165 Slim waists and full skirts, which were to be a feature of post-war fashions, were seen in 1939, even in 'house gowns' in a Chilprufe catalogue a flexible backing. The first patent for a zip was taken out in America in 1914, but, surprisingly, the device that was to become such a wonderful time saver and to answer a classic complaint about one of life's trials being all this buttoning and unbuttoning was slow to develop in America. It first appeared in corsetry there in 1931 and in Britain the 'Lightning' zip arrived in 1933–1934. It was soon being used by leading corset manufacturers. In 1935 salesgirls were advised, in a trade publication, to 'explain its use and operation' to their customers. To start with the zip was heavy and much-taped, and to the post-war years belong its more sophisticated developments, such as self-locking slides and much finer constructions.

The pantie-girdle, which in its many forms was to become a leader in foundationwear, was acclaimed in 1935. 'The pantee corset', said *Corsetry & Underwear* in June of that year, 'is sweeping triumphantly into the best-seller class of leading fashion houses and is destined to make fashion history'. It was a true prophecy. One successful 1935 style was the 'Silcute' by Kestos, a two-way stretch elastic pantie made in pure Lastex yarn, fashioned to shape and with a smooth surface free of seams or bones. There were also many other versions in the immediate pre-war years.

Just before the Second World War broke out, there was evidence of a return to fashions that emphasised the waist. *Vogue* wrote enthusiastically: 'The only thing you must have . . . is a tiny waist, held in if necessary by super-light-weight boned and laced corsets. There isn't a silhouette in Paris that doesn't cave in at the waist'. Also advocated is 'an old-fashioned boned and laced corset, made, by modern magic, light and persuasive as a whisper'. Although the war put an end to that trend, the first real post-war fashion, the Dior 'New Look', did require 'a tiny waist' and was worn with a corset that assisted this. It was as though fashion had been put in a deep freeze for the intervening years.

15

Clothing by Decree, then the New Look and more changes 1939–1960

Nylon, which is the most important innovation in the whole history of underwear, also originated in the immediate pre-war years, although its use in underwear, as in outer clothing and numerous other commodities, is a post-war story.

E.I. Du Pont de Nemours Inc. were the originators of nylon, and they gave it its name (a generic one, coined by them and not based on any existent word). Nylon, a polyamide derived from carbon, oxygen and hydrogen, was the result of a fundamental research programme started by Du Pont in 1927 and carried out by the late Dr Wallace H. Carothers and his staff. The aim of the research was not to create a specific product but to study polymerisation – how and why very small molecules join up and form large ones. By 1930 Dr Carothers and his researchers had discovered that a fibre of extreme tensile strength could be drawn from a treacle-like mass of linear polymers, but years of research followed and Dr Carothers died in 1937, a year before the discovery of nylon was announced by Du Pont in October 1938.

World-wide interest was roused when the Company showed the first ever nylon stockings at the New York World Fair in that year. About 27 million dollars had in the previous eleven years been spent on research and development and fantastic claims were inevitably made for the new nylon, most of which Du Pont had to disclaim. The first nylon stockings were offered for sale to employees of the Company at its experimental station at Wilmington, Delaware, in February 1939. In the same month similar stockings were exhibited at the Golden Gate International Exposition in San Francisco and in March the first public sales took place at a few retail stores at Wilmington. The first large public sales on a country-wide scale were made in October 1939.

The first complete outfit made of nylon was shown at the New York World's Fair in 1940. Nylon apparel then began to appear on the American market in wider variety but in limited quantities. It included

women's lingerie and foundation garments and it was widely acclaimed by the public. Its first heyday, however, was brief, for in December
1941 nylon in America went to war, just as it had done in Britain more
than two years before.

By a strange coincidence nylon, which was to have a profound effect
upon the future of all clothing, was introduced into Britain on 1
January 1940, the day when wartime restrictions first hit the country in
the way which traditionally hurts most – by the introduction of food
rationing.

On this 1 January British Nylon Spinners Ltd, a private company,
with a capital of £300,000 subscribed in equal proportions by ICI Ltd
and Courtaulds Ltd, was formed to manufacture and sell nylon in
Britain. This was possible because Du Pont had granted nylon rights in
Britain to ICI, who in turn granted them to British Nylon Spinners and
Courtaulds.

Needless to say, Britain's first five years' output of the new yarn went
wholly to such vital wartime needs as parachutes, jungle tents, glider
tow-ropes and tarpaulins. For these nylon was an incomparable and
almost incredibly opportune invention, because of its unequalled
strength. British women's first personal experience of nylon came in
the shape of a thin trickle of stockings brought back privately from the
USA in the early war years, mainly by Atlantic-crossing business men.
The sheer-clad legs of the lucky few were the bitter envy of their less
fortunate sisters.

The stockings aroused such envy not solely because of the marvels of
nylon. Stockings soon began to be in short supply. Food shortages were
inevitably accompanied by other shortages in both the materials and
the labour needed for civilian production. As early as spring 1940
controls were, for instance, introduced restricting the amount of
corsetry available for civilian use to 75 per cent of the pre-war level of
the manufacturer concerned.

On 7 June 1941 clothes rationing came into force in Britain, which
meant that a fixed quota of clothing coupons was issued to every man,
woman and child at decreed intervals, that a coupon value was put
upon almost every item of attire and that the requisite coupons had to
be surrendered for every purchase. There were only a few very minor
exceptions, mainly accessories, such as ties, collars, handkerchiefs,
scarves and gloves. Furnishing and black-out materials were exempt,
and were put to ingenious use by some women especially for dressing
gowns and underwear.

More drastic in some ways in its effect on fashion was the introduction of the Utility Scheme, announced in March 1942 by the Government. This, with its soon familiar CC41 symbol, was the first instance
in modern history of what came near to clothing by decree because

The Last Lingerie

from America
— for a time

Sheer, luxurious, silk milanese nightgowns, with adorable puff sleeves. Edged with Val. lace. Launders in a flash. Peach, ice blue. All sizes. American.
25/9

Daintily embroidered sprays on excellent quality locknit. Beautifully fitting bodice and ample width. Peach, rose, ivory, marine blue. This is the only garment on this page that is not American make. Outsizes, 2/- extra.

166 Goodbye to glamour – the elegance of underwear in 1940, just before restrictions began to affect the corset and lingerie trade

under it Government rules and regulations controlled the substance, shape, design and price of almost everything that everyone wore, regardless of age, rank, wealth or poverty. Regulations also specified the amount of material which could be used for every garment, the kind of buttons, collars, cuffs, the shape and number of pockets to be permitted. Manufacturers had to use approved fabrics and their profit margins were controlled. At first the scheme applied to 50 per cent of all production but later this was increased to 85 per cent. Though the remaining 15 per cent was unrestricted in selling price and in the nature of the materials, styles and amounts of materials were controlled.

Where underwear for women was concerned, the wartime regulations hit hard by the ban imposed on all trimmings, embroidery, lace and other similar embellishments, as well as by the limitations set on design and the lack of choice of materials. Many manufacturers found themselves caught up in concentration schemes with others who would normally be competitors, as a proportion of factories was taken over for war production. Distinctive characteristics of individual companies were therefore diluted or lost. It also became increasingly difficult to obtain the innumerable components required for the production of clothing even on the new restricted scale. In corsetry, for instance, steel supports were for obvious reasons in short supply as steel was needed for more important purposes, and unsatisfactory fibre 'bones' had to be used. Imports of rubber for corsetry and underwear were also hit.

Women's stockings were hit by the war to an extent that caused more widespread inconvenience and discomfort than most of the new regulations. Only rayon stockings were permitted under the Utility Scheme and as more factories were taken over for wartime needs and both men and women employees were called up for service, the scarcity of all kinds of stockings became acute. So too was the scarcity of coupons that could be spared for them. Many women started going bare-legged in both summer and winter, even in town and on quite formal occasions. To do so was startling at that less permissive time. Leg make-up was introduced to make the nudity less obvious and ingenious women painted mock-seams with soft black pencils up the backs of their legs, to simulate vanished full-fashioned seams.

In corsetry both in Britain and in America one beam of light shone through the darkness created by the low standards imposed on manufacturers and their fabric suppliers by Government departments. In Britain women in the services and the hosts of others required to do 'men's work' and to stand for long hours at factory benches were vocal on the fact that they now needed good corsetry more than ever for physical support. These clamorous voices eventually reached the ears of the Government early in 1944 through a recently established body, The Corset Guild of Great Britain, formed in 1943 by retail shop buyers who were the direct recipients of the public's pleas. With the support of a number of leading corset manufacturers, who had joined them in the Guild, they presented at 10 Downing Street a petition on behalf of British women. This resulted in March 1944 in corsetry being classified under what was known as an 'Essential Works Order'. This enabled the corset industry to maintain certain standards and to produce garments that were functionally designed and capable of being comfortable and providing support for the figure.

In America similar agitation arose, and there too it achieved a successful result. Women in America had the advantage of a staunch advocate in high office – Miss Mary Anderson, Director of the Women's Bureau of the Department of Labour. She declared corsets to be essential to the performance of women's tasks in the war effort, pointing out that fatigue was the main reason why women frequently left their war jobs in the USA. To provide good corsets, which would reduce fatigue, was therefore necessary to the vigorous maintenance of the war effort.

After the war America, less subject than Britain to prolonged shortages and general stringency, secured a considerable lead in many fields of civilian production. Not least of these were those of corsetry and underwear, where both in materials and in design Britain lagged behind for many years. How long the wartime restrictions lasted is apt to be forgotten. They continued long after hostilities had ended. The scheme for clothes rationing in general went on until March 1949 and it was not until then that any real easing began. Even after that some restrictions remained. The Utility Scheme, aimed at ensuring the production of necessary clothing requirements under price-controlled conditions lasted until 1952 and the subsequent controls exercised by the D scheme over manufacturing and selling continued until 1955. Within this elaborate framework of clothing restrictions only very limited quantities of garments of higher quality and price were permitted for many years and to find them was a kind of treasure hunt. The process of relaxation came slowly.

After the war nylon stockings which, as already described, had made their first appearance in America in 1938, began to be manufactured in Britain, but they remained in short supply throughout the immediate post-war years. It was some time before British Nylon Spinners were able to produce the fine quality yarns needed for stockings and in addition much of the early output was earmarked by the Government for the export drive needed to rehabilitate Britain's trade. Kayser Bondor – the name given to the early Full-Fashioned Hosiery Company in 1940 – were the first to manufacture 15 denier nylon stockings in Britain, but in 1950 they stated that 'it will be many years yet before the home market can be satisfied and the price reduced'. The cost of installing new machinery for the new stockings kept prices up at first. In 1950, however, it was also said by the company that 'fine gauge full-fashioned stockings are an essential part of the modern woman's wardrobe all over the world. Kayser Bondor meet this need with stockings of nylon, pure silk and chiffon lisle'. The nylon ones went ahead with such force that in a short time the very word stockings was being supplanted by the new name 'nylons' in current usage, just as the elastic girdle had become a 'roll-on' in the 1920s. The name stuck for years – until tights began to take over the function and the name.

Foundationwear was enjoying a boom at this time and an Economic Intelligence Unit Survey showed that sales of foundation garments in Britain practically doubled between 1948 and 1958. It was the last chapter of a long tradition of good dressing which called for top-to-toe immaculate grooming. The slim, closely waisted tailor-made suit was the main item for conventional occasions and through the 1950s it was completed by a good hat, perfect gloves, impeccable high heeled shoes, matching handbag and probably a slim umbrella. Evening dress also conformed to strict rules, formally décolleté, slim of body, full of skirt. The leaders in both areas of fashion were the top couturiers and it was significant that in the mid-1950s the still enthroned hierarchy of London fashion leaders, the members of the Incorporated Society of London Fashion Designers, formed a close and open alliance with the corset trade by including Berlei, a leading manufacturer, among the associate members it allied to itself in order to present a complete fashion picture – and to aid its own struggling finances. From this time it held combined seasonal fashion 'spectaculars' in which were shown

167 *(left)* The kind of foundation chosen by top couturiers of the 1950s to be worn at their fashion shows

168 *(right)* Longline strapless bra of 1952 in nylon voile, lace and elastic

not only the highlights of their own collections but also furs, stockings, jewellery, knitwear, hats and foundations. In the shows of individual houses credits were given to the makers of the corsets worn by the model girls. Hardy Amies anticipated future taste by recording in his descriptive lists of his clothes that under them were 'stays by Berlei' – even then he disliked the words 'corset' and 'foundation'. Evening foundations were given exotic names, among then Pink Champagne, Merry Widow, Charade. These were presented at fashion shows as visible tops to dresses with swirling skirts by John Cavanagh and under a ten-yard wide evening coat by Victor Stiebel. The model girls glittered with jewellery, usually diamonds. These visible under-pinnings were in some cases called Torsolettes to avoid the unpopular connotations of corsets. Bras were also given exotic names; one was known as Renoir, while others included Pink Ice, Sweet and Low, French Accent and Camellia. A range of bras and girdles was called Sasha, another Sarong.

So prestigious was the corset that in the 1950s the whole nation was alerted to it by the event called National Corset Week. It sounds incredible now, but there was about this time a spate of such weeks, devoted to promoting sales of various items of apparel, including gloves and millinery. It was claimed that there were about 1,000 shop window displays of corsets in shops and stores all over the country, during the first National Corset Week of 1952. In 1957 there was an impressive inaugural luncheon for the event at a London hotel, followed by a Forum at which trade experts answered questions from the press on problems of figures and corsetry. Alison Adburgham recorded it in *Punch* on 6 March 1957, with her characteristic gentle astringency: 'The contemporary corset has to be seen to be believed, and that it shall be seen is the earnest intention of the promoters of National Corsetry Week, which is now in full swing. This fascinating fixture includes shop window displays in every town, and it is unlikely that those will be passed by with averted eyes. For the art and craft of corsetry has reached its finest flowering in the new materials of today, and there is, in addition, the fresh interest in the feminine silhouette evoked by Christian Dior's A-line – the most significant cipher since the S-curve of the Edwardian Gaiety Girl. Even the professionally un-concerned must be aware that what goes on underneath the A-line is of fundamental importance'. It was – the National Corset Weeks were a notable success both in the displays that proclaimed them and the rising corset sales that accrued.

The process of easing women out of wartime restrictions was given a bold impetus by the introduction of the famous 'New Look' in Paris by Christian Dior in Spring 1947 in the first collection shown at his newly established couture house. While cloth was still rationed he put yards

169 'New Look' petticoat and matching boned corselette, 1948

of it into full, flowing, below-calf-length skirts, extending to twelve inches from the ground and replacing the shorter, tubular styles that had been established for years. Instead of the current square-shouldered jackets with lightly defined waists he presented a short jacket with rounded shoulders and a nipped-in waist. The padding hitherto used for the very wide, squared shoulders now gave shape to the slightly flared basques of the new Dior jackets.

In spite of the loud disapproval of the British authorities (headed by Sir Harold Wilson as president of the Board of Trade), and protests from the patriotic and the serious-minded, the new line was instantly and widely adopted in Britain. Fashion came to life again, and designers, both in couture houses and among the wholesale manufacturers, seized upon it with the heady excitement that came from years of frustration and repression. Though the initial extreme New Look was soon modified for general wear, it established a trend that lasted for nearly ten years, until the mid-1950s.

Under the new full skirts went voluminous petticoats and in the first enthusiasm these were often brightly coloured and frilled. In many cases they were trophies rescued from grandmother's attic. There was a fine *cachet* in letting a flash of scarlet or bright green silk be glimpsed as these busy, active post-war women swung onto buses and trains in their unsuitable but exhilarating new flowing skirts.

To make the most of the newly revived small waist, the 'waspie' appeared. This was a short corset, sometimes only five or six inches deep, made of rigid material with elastic inserts, little bones and sometimes back lacing. It was shaped sharply into the waist and was worn very tight, in the manner of the despised Victorians. Other corsets of the time also showed an hour-glass look. The idea was not, however, widely adopted or long-lived. The very fashionable essayed it. Model girls groaningly laced or pulled themselves into tight 'waspies' for fashion shows, but once the parade was over off came the new menace: their corsets were killing them. Usually the short waspie was worn over the familiar roll-on or a light pantie-girdle.

From this time underwear in general was transformed by the use of nylon, which began to be used in increasing quantities. There is a curious footnote to its wartime rôle in the advertisement in April 1946 of a famous brassière company which refers to 'parachute fabric into Partos brassières, creating beauty and with their scientific design ensuring lasting satisfaction'. Nylon was, however, being 'demobbed' and in 1947 it was first shown at the British Industries Fair, where the new underwear fabrics made from it were described as 'a beauty and a revolution'. Nylon foundation garments and lingerie were included in the garments shown, among the underwear being items of the warp-knit type material which, as nylon tricot, was to occupy a dominant

170   Boned back-lacing 'waspie' in nylon and satin with elastic satin side panels, 1948

171   1950 version of the corselette with long, smooth line

172 Calf-length nylon slip trimmed at bust and hem with lace and with pleated nylon frill

position in the underwear world from that time onwards until the present day.

Nylon did indeed introduce a new era in the underwear world. Delectable, gossamer-light, hard-wearing underwear that could be rinsed out and drip-dried in an hour or two, with no need of ironing, was now available on the mass market, at prices that would previously have bought only coarse and unattractive garments. A wide choice of nylon materials now came into existence, in different weights as well as in various knitted and woven constructions. In the knitted type, the weight and texture were and still are indicated in two ways. The word denier, also used for elastic nets, means the weight in grammes of 9,000 metres of synthetic fibre in the form of a continuous filament. Deniers can vary from 15 for stockings to as much as 140 to 1,120 for heavy stable and elastic materials. Another variation is described as gauge, here again for elastics as well as nylon. It means the number of ends of the yarn on a knitting machine to each inch of fabric. The higher the gauge the finer the material.

The attraction and availability of nylon and its inexpensiveness were so great that underwear, which had hitherto been even more suscept-ible to social and fashion snobbery than had outerwear, now became almost classless. The new nylons were not suitable for hand-sewing, so the vogue for hand-made silk, satin and crêpe de Chine underwear among elegant women practically ended. Underwear became truly democratic, in which respect it preceded a similar trend in outerwear that has become manifest in recent years.

Although by today's standards the underwear of the late '40s and early '50s seems voluminous and fussy, the introduction of nylon and of the mass-production methods that were stimulated by the rising demand for what was now a machine-made article, progressively led to simpler and more functional styles. Briefs, in various kinds of nylon and in many designs, superseded the more elaborate French knickers of pre-war glamour. Cami-knickers went out of fashion and the simpler slip was worn. Underwear, which had been cut on the cross when woven silks were used, was now usually cut on the straight, as befitted the knitted fabrics that were mainly used.

At the same time that it was introducing a new concept in underwear, nylon also had a profound effect on foundationwear. The cottons, brochés, satins and other fabrics previously needed to ensure control in rigid garments or parts of garments could now be replaced by light-weight nylon taffeta, nylon voile, nylon marquisette and similar materials. As strong as natural ones but immeasurably lighter, they were being used in corsetry by 1947 and they contributed an important step towards the glamorising of foundationwear and the creation of lightweight garments capable of providing degrees of control hitherto

173 Power net pantie with lightly boned satin front, worn with nylon bra, 1948

available only by the use of formidable fabrics. Even more important was the contribution made by nylon elastic net towards the lightening of foundationwear.

Important too was the great improvement in elasticised materials brought about by the production of them on the warp knitting machine, which began in the early 1950s. Originally bobbinet machines were used for these fabrics and subsequently various other lace machines were also employed. The original patent for two-way stretch fabrics made on warp knitting looms was taken out in the nineteenth century, but it was not until after the Second World War that the high production potential of these machines was recognised. Their development started in the USA, and reached Britain in the early 1950s. The main advantages of the warp knitting machine, previously used for locknit materials, were far greater speed and far longer runs of material. Where previously the length of elastic net that could be woven was limited by the amount of elastic that could be run on – and off – a bobbin, the new process meant that several hundred yards of material could be produced continuously, as opposed to the previous fifteen or sixteen yards. Production capacity for two-way stretch fabrics increased enormously and also resulted in much cheaper fabrics.

The full effect of this on corset design and manufacture was not, however, realised until about 1954–1955, when the fully elasticised foundation garment broke through into the popular market. A pioneer in this development was the famous 'Little X' by Silhouette, the first two-way stretch corset to be marketed in Britain under a brand name of its own. It was rapidly followed by a series of other branded all-elastic garments. From that time onwards the conception of the all-elastic corset was firmly established.

The item of underwear with the liveliest history in the post-war years is the brassière. It had, it will be recalled, gone through quite a variety of developments in the '30s, first in the Mae West era and later, when the Scarlett O'Hara bra had quite a vogue in America. This lead from Hollywood characterised fashion developments after the war, when American films dominated the entertainment world. In addition, America's briefer participation in the war and her more rapid material recovery gave her, among other things, a good lead in the development of the man-made fibres that were particularly important in this connection.

Reasons given for the exploitation of the bosom in post-war years include the suggestion that 'In the hungry post-1939 world, as in the hungry post-Napoleonic world . . . the female breast is the obvious symbol of nourishment'. Another view is that it was simply a shift of the erogenous zone. Dior's 'New Look' of 1947 emphasised the bosom, together with other feminine curves, so it was not strange that women everywhere became very bra-conscious. American film stars in the '40s and even in the '50s are credited with having risen to fame by virtue of the splendour of their bosoms rather than of acting talents and it was declared that 'one American lady was selected to star in a popular American television programme entirely on account of her oversize bosom'.

How serious the correct fashionable shape of the bust was is instanced by a dramatic episode in Harold Robbins' best-selling novel of 1961, *The Carpet Baggers*. Believed to have its origin in fact, it tells how a very curvaceous Hollywood actress, about to be launched on her first starring rôle, was encased in a brassière that made her into a straight line, and then in a harness-style bra that was little better. Unfortunately, without a bra, her ample bosom bounced. The fashion designer revolted, declaring she was 'a designer, not a structural engineer'. That gave the director the vital clue. An aeronautical engineer was sent for and, with the aid of calipers to measure the depth and circumference, and calculations to find the point of stress, he designed a bra on the suspension principle in a little over an hour. The result was perfect and sensationally successful.

The most popular type of bra in the '50s was known as the 'sweater girl' bra, which reached its peak (literally) about 1957. Inspired by film star Jane Russell, its aim was to create an exaggerated high, pointed bosom – an achievement in which nature was almost wholly replaced by artifice. These bras were shaped to sharp points, stiffened and built up. For those to whom Nature had been niggardly, 'falsies' or padded bras of this shape were the answer. 'The ideal aimed at', says Pearl Binder, a well-known writer on the history of fashion, 'is two spiked cones never before seen in Europe and related only to the female form in African sculpture'.

This trend was so generally followed that in 1955 leading corset buyers attending a conference of the Corset Guild of Great Britain at Manchester dwelt on the fact that three out of every four women were at that time wearing 'cuties' and 'falsies' – both descriptions of the artificial bust-maker. All sorts of bust-improvers were advertised and displayed in shop windows, including pneumatic busts that could be inflated at will, like a balloon.

Wiring was revived about 1945, and though at first hard, uncomfortable and suspected in some quarters of being dangerous to the breast, it was in a few years flat, light, well-covered and perfectly comfortable to wear. Circular stitching was widely used to achieve fashionable protruding, pointed bust cups.

Another development of the '50s was the strapless bra, which was very widely worn with the strapless evening dresses which remained in

174   The pointed bra of the 1950s, its effect created by circular stitching. With it 'Next-to-Nothing' nylon net belt. Twilfit

175   Strapless bras had a great vogue in the 1950s

vogue for many years. Such dresses usually had full skirts, which were held out either by wiring, in a revival of the crinoline, or by petticoats of stiffened materials, including tiers of nylon net. The very full crinolines were mainly worn on very formal occasions and by the wealthy and fashionable, and the Royal Ladies wore them with great faithfulness for many years.

There was, also, in the late 1950s, a dominating 'young' fashion for short, very full daytime skirts of the dirndl type. Under these were worn petticoats of almost ballerina fullness, belling out with rows upon rows of frills and lace. Sometimes they even reverted to the old-fashioned embroidered or lace-trimmed starched cotton. Sometimes they were of stiffened nylon net. Under them briefs were functionally plain, but bras still aimed at uplift, and the bosom was emphasised by

176   Flaring petticoat in nylon with frills made of 50 yards of lace-edged nylon net, 1959

Firm control for the fuller figure

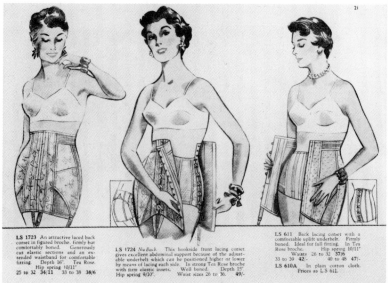

177 *(left)* Formidable foundationwear was still worn in the 1950s by women with heavy figures. Long bras and front-lacing corsets gave the control that was still desired. Twilfit, 1957

178 *(right)* The heavier figure of 1957 wore a corset with an underbelt. 'Liberty' by Symington

padding and wiring, though this was moderating towards the end of the 1950s. In corsetry the step-in, in elastic net, was favoured by the young. The corselette was in considerable favour, but, in spite of the stimulus given to designers by nylon and improvements in the making of elastic nets, it was still a fairly heavy garment. So were the numerous functional girdles that controlled curves and trimmed outlines under fashions that were much more formal and figure-fitting than those of the late '60s and early '70s.

16

The Youth Revolution. Today's invisible underwear, and underwear that goes everywhere 1960–1978

Just what was the start of the Youth Revolution, which was so greatly to affect fashion, outer and under, from the 1960s, is in some doubt. The Teddy Boys of the later 1940s and 1950s were the first visible signs of it to attract widespread public attention; the accompanying Teddy Girl's black seamed nylons, a breakaway from accepted fashion to the Edwardian theme of her partner's eccentric outfit, were probably the first sign of girl-participation in the coming trend. More significant, and about the same time, was the Baby Doll nightdress, the thigh-high garment, with accompanying brief bloomers, which became a fashionable craze among the young in the mid-1950s and continued to flourish for many years. It had a vigorous revival in 1977.

Foundationwear was also quick off the mark to meet what was seen as an important growth area of the fashion market. By 1960 Kayser Bondor were running a Teenage Advice Bureau to help schoolgirls with their underwear problems and were producing a special range of bras, suspender belts and girdles for adolescent figures. In the same year Berlei acquired the British rights to Teenform, an American range of the same garments made by a company which concentrated exclusively on the needs of the growing girl, from the age of 10 or 11 onwards – the 'between-ager', younger than the teenager who already received considerable attention. Teenform was selling nine million garments a year in the USA and at this time was extending its activities to Europe. Manufacturers' booklets advocating the wearing of bras from pre-teen years were widely circulated through schools in a campaign that tied up youthful grooming and health with the merchandise concerned.

These were all light-weight, easy garments, but with a fashion look that had hitherto been missing from schoolgirl underwear. They catered for the new, assertive generation of post-war girls who had minds of their own about what they wore. So far as foundationwear in general was concerned this meant that girls grew up with garments

179 Teenform roll-on and bra, introduced in the 1960s by Berlei

180 Today's version of the junior bra is 'Girltime', made in a plunge version as well as the basic everyday one

that were light and comfortable; they would therefore expect similar qualities in their adult foundationwear. Just as the eighteenth-century small girl's 'trowsers' led the way to women adopting drawers early in the next century and the small boy's skeleton suit led to men taking to trousers, so the youthful foundationwear of the 1960s affected all foundationwear.

Before fashion trends could develop in this direction there came, opportunely, another, and the last to date, of the big developments in fibres and fabrics which brought about revolutionary changes in underwear and foundationwear. In this case, as before, the new arrival was a man-made fibre and its influence on foundationwear was as great as that of the earlier nylon on underwear in general.

The innovation, still in its heyday and still developing, was man-made elastics. Commercially described at the time of their invention as Spandex fibres, they contain no natural rubber at all. They became known for a time as elastomerics, but in 1976 were given the EEC name of elastane. Lycra, which dominates this group of fibres, is, like nylon, much lighter than its natural counterpart. Weight by weight, it is about three times as powerful as rubber elastic, so it has opened up a new conception of light-weight, yet controlling foundationwear.

Lycra, like nylon, was invented in the Du Pont USA laboratories, this time in the course of research aimed at finding ways of producing a fibre that would have the elastic qualities of rubber but at the same time be a true textile. This project led to the discovery of what was known in its experimental stages as Fibre K. It was introduced for trade evaluation in the USA in 1958. In October 1959 the trade name 'Lycra' was announced. A pilot plant started producing Lycra in America and foundationwear manufacturers began to put it into production so as to test the product and its potential market. In December 1960 fabric made from the new fibre was described in *Corsetry & Underwear* in Britain, and in the same month Warner Bros launched out with a full-page British trade advertisement for their first garment 'in the new Lycra fabric', a step-in called 'Little Godiva'. In the next month their 'Merry Widow' evening corselette with Lycra was introduced into Britain.

181   The original 'Birthday Suit', 1961

In 1961 Warners again made foundationwear history by introducing into Britain their 'Birthday Suit', a close-fitting, smoothly knitted pantie-corselette, using Lycra, boneless, almost seamless and rather like a swimsuit. Made in sizes 34 to 38, it weighed a mere three ounces but cost the considerable sum of 8½ guineas. It was the forerunner of the 'nude look' that was to make headlines a few years later and also of many future body stockings and similar garments of the late '60s and early '70s. All of these were the culmination of a new simplification of foundationwear made possible by Lycra.

In January 1962 it was said that 'Spandex fibres are currently bringing about a revolution in the foundation garment industry' and in that year an American plant went into commercial production. In November 1962 Du Pont celebrated this in London by holding a spectacular parade of foundationwear that used Lycra. At the end of 1963 'everything is coming up in Lycra for the Spring'.

In 1963 a plant for manufacturing Lycra fibre was built at Dordrecht in the Netherlands, mainly to supply the European market, including Britain, which had up to then been dependent upon imports from the USA or Canada. In August 1969, when Lycra had become a mainstay of British fashion foundationwear further production was started at Du Pont's plant at Maydown, Londonderry, which was already engaged in producing Orlon acrylic fibre. The major part of the Lycra made here was for the supply of the United Kingdom and European Free Trade Area countries.

For the first few years, foundationwear with Lycra mostly made use of nets, produced in a large variety of deniers, as were natural rubber elastic fabrics and nylon. Such fabrics did not consist entirely of Lycra, any more than their conventional counterparts were wholly of rubber elastic. The proportion of Lycra (which usually ranged from 15 per cent to 40 per cent) was dependent upon the amount of stretch required.

The new fabrics containing Lycra were comfortably supple in

182   1970 pantie-corselette in Lycra, by Berlei

texture. The lightness of the fibre was a prime attraction and its special qualities included the possession of from two to four times the break-strength of natural elastic thread of the same denier and up to twice the recovery power. It was also claimed to have better resistance to abrasion. It resisted perspiration, oils and lotions and was unharmed by detergents. It could be dyed. Unlike conventional rubber elastic, Lycra could be knitted into fabrics in its bare state as well as covered, and this meant that it opened the way to new fabric constructions, which were soon to be developed. From the start it meant a new era of light-weight control for foundationwear.

The general trend of foundations from the '60s to the present time has been progressively towards increasingly natural shaping. It has aimed at smoothing and controlling the figure and improving on nature without exaggerating natural curves or introducing any artificiality. Where muscles are weak, where the figure is flabby and has lost its ideal tautness, the foundation garment of today aims to take over and persuade it back towards what it should be.

The 'youth explosion' rocketed in the 1960s, given impetus by the post-war 'bulge' in the birth-rate and by the 'never had it so good' Macmillan era when the pay packets of the new teenage young also rocketed. The most blatant self-assertion of the girl of this period, the mid-'60s, was the startling fashion of the mini-skirt when, for the first time in modern history and probably since the girl athletes of classical Sparta, skirts rose high above the knees and often right up to the thighs. In terms of underwear, the traditional cover-up, there was very little left to cover up or conceal. No conventional version of the corset could be worn under the mini-skirt, nor could any accepted style of petticoat. Knickers had to be the briefest of briefs. The most dramatic change, however, was that stockings, part of feminine attire for at least half a dozen centuries, received the first intimation of their dismissal. Nothing could make their visible tops, the equally visible holding suspenders and the gap in between, look becoming or even bearable under the new mini. After a brief, disastrous period when girls strove to bridge the gap with tightly pulled up stockings, tights took over and, with briefs, became for many of the young the only underwear they wanted. The girdle, pantie-girdle, corset or whatever had been worn did not go with the new style and they all began to have the bad image that was to beset them in the 1970s. They were worn only to conceal figure defects, not as the enhancers of the natural shape which they had come to be.

Tights are generally assumed to have been invented after the mini-skirt, but this was not so. Apart from the long-existing ballet dancer's tights, which provided a prototype, Morleys had been making them since 1960, but for warmth, not fashion. They were thick, usually of wool, in bright colours, and were intended as sportswear. Contrary to general belief, tights did not come in overnight. Advertisements for stockings continued to appear regularly in fashion magazines until 1969, when there came a prominent full-page advertisement announcing that 'Annabella is not wearing stockings. She's wearing something much better, Charnos Hold-me-Tights'. In that year tights accounted for 160.9 million pairs out of a total of over 470 million of stockings and tights produced. Within a very few years they were dominating the whole market and have done so ever since.

As the mini-skirt was introduced as, and continued to be, a youthful fashion, born of a youthful desire to be different and to find the answer to its own specific needs, it could not by itself oust stockings from the whole market. Practically no one over 25 wore it, so the sales of tights meant that the latter were also wearing tights under their more discreet skirts. Increasingly they rid themselves of the unsightly suspenders, the drag on their corsets, glad to know that, however they moved and however wildly the winds blew, there would be no revelation of bare thighs and the gap above the stocking top. The idea that one should look as trim and attractive underneath as when fully dressed was born and it was new to the underwear picture.

The change was not an instant one. It took until 1976 for most corset manufacturers to stop supplying removable suspenders with pantie-girdles and pantie-corselettes, which were becoming the top selling styles of foundations. Most surprising was a great drop in fully fashioned stockings sales. Seamless tights – and seamless stockings too – now clung as closely to the legs as seamed ones and had a more casual look, which suited the fashion trend of the times. The fully fashioned stocking, once regarded as essential to the well-dressed woman, dropped from holding 72 per cent of the stocking market in 1964 to holding a mere 5 per cent of tights and stockings in 1971. Today it only just survives, having to be sought out by the dwindling tiny minority of older women faithful to tradition.

The mini-skirt, like the short skirts of the 1920s, which were long by comparison, lasted for a very short time, from about 1965 to 1970, and was, unlike the earlier version, never generally worn. Yet it made a greater impact than any other fashion of recent times upon the public attention, was more fiercely liked and hated, added a new word to the language and left underwear greatly diminished. To wear only a bra and tights under outer clothes became increasingly usual and many of the young continued to do so even when they were no longer very young.

Manufacturers of corsetry and underwear met this challenge by various means. They concentrated on developing new and more attractive bras, which were in great demand, and Gossard, who subse-

quently gave up corset manufacture after a long and successful career in this field, introduced in 1969 their Wonderbra, which became a best seller and remains so today. Other companies devoted themselves to making full use of recent fabric developments. In the late 1960s and early 1970s tricot types of Lycra had been evolved. With the texture and appearance of soft satin they opened the way to the production of co-ordinates in foundationwear and underwear, because the same look could be achieved in stretch fabrics with Lycra and matching stable ones, either in plain colours or in the prints which were having a considerable vogue at this time and were a novelty. Though co-ordinated innerwear had been introduced in 1961, it had till now been limited because of the impossibility of matching elasticised materials to plain ones. Now complete sets of bras, pantie-girdles, corselettes, briefs and slips could be produced with stretch where wanted. They were much in demand, with new prints being evolved each season. With falling sales of functional corsetry, manufacturers began to diversify into this style of merchandise, which was to develop still further in the future as the demand for traditional foundationwear dropped. Other corset companies took to making swimwear, which in fact very closely resembled current underwear, and also diversified into leisurewear.

It was said that the severe winter of 1969 killed the mini-skirt and sent its wearers headlong to the other extreme – the ground-length 'maxi' skirt and, even more, coat which have had an intermittent life for some years as part of the increasing variety and confusion of fashion in an age which carries permissiveness into all aspects of its attire.

183   The Wonderbra introduced in 1969, said to be the top-selling bra in the world, here in its 1977 version

184   Lycra led the way to co-ordinates, seen here in the printed tricot popular from 1968–1971

Women, the research claimed, never had liked girdles and had submitted to them despite resentment about restriction and discomfort because there was no option. Wearing a girdle was until recent years 'almost a legal requirement'. Everyone did. Now, given the choice by casual dress and tights, 'by "go-natural" life styles and relaxed social standards, women *en masse* decided no'.

They put forward reasons for doing so. They believed that wearing girdles made muscles lazy and harmed circulation. They kept their weight down by dieting and exercise or else they lived with the figure they had, being able in today's fragmented fashion structure to find a style that suited every size and shape. This trend had grown steadily since 1970, but was strongest among the young, the working woman and the higher income-bracket woman who were the mainstay of the apparel industries.

On another level girdles were looked on as 'a symbol of male chauvinism', arbitrary dictates of fashion authorities who were no longer respected. They were also looked on as cheats, a way of pretending to be something you were not, of conning your man with something you couldn't get away with. Girdles, it was said, also turned men off; they liked their wives and girl friends 'to feel like women'. They liked a behind with a wiggle. A girdle therefore became an admission of advancing age or loss of muscle tone, to be avoided as long as possible and classed by some of the young with false teeth.

Research, however, showed that this was not all the picture. Women admitted that they were not all Venuses, that it helped to have their figures smoothed and shaped, their derrières moulded a little into a higher, rounder line. They admitted that the special occasion dress, the tailored suit, was improved by something under it to help nature. It was, however, up to the manufacturer to produce and market what was needed, to sell women not a garment but a shape, a look.

One fact was that what women disliked most of all was not a garment but a name. They detested the words corset, foundation, girdle, control. These all had a bad, outmoded image. The corset's centuries-long service to fashion, the importance of the foundation when the fashionable shape was the very essence of elegance and elegance was the surest way to social confidence – these meant nothing now. Corset departments were revamped and renamed Foundationwear departments, but that did not help much. A host of new names were tried out in the hope that the garment would outdo the rose and by any other name not smell but be much more sweet. Corsets were called body fashions, bodygarments, bodysuits, clothes smoothers, intimate apparel, innerwear, outerwear enhancers, shape-suits, under-fashions. Girdles were called, with bras, innerwear co-ordinates, bra sets, lingerie sets; by themselves pants smoothers and skin enhancers. The trade publication which for many years flourished under the name *Corsetry and Underwear* prefaced *Foundationwear* to its title, then in 1977 changed its name to *Body Lines*. The Leicester Polytechnic's Department of Foundationwear and Lingerie Design, the only source of such specialised training in Europe, became the Contour Fashions Department in 1976. The principal, Mrs Frances Alcock, said that when the course entitled students to receive the degree of BA (Hons) its name was regarded as undignified and unworthy of this distinction. The new description has since then come to be used by trade and public as one of the acceptable alternatives to the hated word corset.

In spite of this it was clear that something different had to be produced to make foundationwear acceptable.

By the mid-1970s fashion was more insistent than ever on comfort, a natural shape and softly textured outerwear, with particular preferences for soft, knitted weaves and sheer, clinging fabrics. Foundationwear of the traditional kind reached a new low because its existence was apparent. The answer to the problem came in moulding, which meant, on its first appearance, the introduction of seamless, one-piece bras and panties, invisible in wear, though still carrying out foundationwear's traditional rôle of improving the natural figure.

The first patents for moulding processes for bras were taken out in 1935 and 1940, but little progress was made in the next 35 years so far as the consumer was concerned. Moulding was a revolution in clothing technology which called for co-operation between garment designers, fabric manufacturers and technical engineers. The processes involved the development of thermoplastic fabrics, pioneered in England by Margaret Disher, collaborating with Tootal, from the late 1960s, and also developed about the same time in Czechoslovakia (for men's slacks) and in Japan (for women's dresses).

Mould techniques involving high temperature (400 degrees F) service plastic tooling had been required by the automotive and aerospace industries for many years, but their employment for women's underwear was something new and revolutionary. They seemed, however, to offer new hope for foundation and underwear manufacturers. Bras and panties were a 'natural' as a first step in this direction, because they called for only shallow moulding, while larger garments would need deep, more complex moulding.

Different fabrics, textures, deniers and fibres needed different moulding specifications, but it was established that synthetic thermoplastic yarns could be produced from nylon, polyester and heat-settable elastane in various blends and weaves. L.H. Heijman of Amsterdam developed in the early 1970s what is believed to be the first commercially available automatic method of moulding and cutting out brassière cups or complete brassière fronts from a continuous roll of

booming at all levels from luxury boutiques to chain stores. They came in all styles, colours, materials and most of them were pretty and decorative, some positively elegant and glamorous. A great number of them were due to stray out of the bedroom, to be bought as leisurewear, to be seized on by the young as evening dresses. In printed cottons they went to the beach or turned up as sun dresses in the summer. They usually cost less and were often more attractive and enterprising than official outerwear. The dressing gown in its turn also moved out of its former domain and in addition to being a housecoat was, more elegantly, a leisure gown, for evenings at home, even for entertaining or going visiting.

The current 'anything goes' mood of fashion made such changes of purpose natural, perhaps inevitable. But there were also other, more

196 Call it a nightdress, call it a party dress; flower-sprigged cotton and polyester. With puff sleeves and high waist, scoop neckline and frilled hem, it is more likely to go dancing than to bed. Kayser, spring 1978.

practical lines of reasoning. One original function of underwear, made of washable cotton or linen, was to protect the body from outerwear which could not be washed or dry-cleaned and, conversely, to protect outerwear, often costly, from bodies which could not enjoy the daily bath. Today's clothing is nearly all easy-care and drip-dry, welcomed by the washing machine. Dry-cleaning is readily available. So are daily baths. There is therefore no need to distinguish between outer and under garments. Secondly, from Elizabethan times, as fashion became increasingly elaborate, underwear had contributed to the artificial shaping of the body by which women and, for a considerable time, men too, sought to improve on nature. Now the figure-smoothing

Lycra can be woven into the tweed of trousers or top, even in jeans. The bra-dress has had quite a vogue in recent years. The jump-suit for casual wear can be a complete outfit, outer and inner combined, and was one of 1978's newest nightwear vogues as well as daytime wear.

In 1950 the Cunningtons, most exhaustive of all costume historians, drew back from tracing the course of underwear after 1939 and, feeling that 'a revolution in underclothes seems imminent', suggested that the new synthetic fabrics might well mean that 'underclothing is dispensed with entirely'. That has not happened, but today's prophet would be

197 Meant for a double life: frilly nightdress and lounge pyjamas, 1977

198 The newest jump-suit, described as 'for jumping into bed or staying up late', in smoky blue Celon trimmed with grey lace, for the young and trendy. Kayser, spring 1978

199 Pop-over housecoat in Aztec stripes, for leisurewear and evenings at home and certainly not to be looked on as a dressing gown. Kayser, 1977

halted by the difficulty of defining what is underwear and what is outerwear. At one and the same time underwear has taken over and has itself been taken over. But whatever happens to it in the future the chain of continuity which persisted through many centuries has been broken and there can be no going back.

UK Bibliography

ADBURGHAM, ALISON, *View of Fashion*, Allen & Unwin, 1966
Aglaia, John Heddon, 1893–1894
ALLEN, AGNES, *The Story of Clothes*, Faber & Faber, 1955
ARNOLD, JANET, *Patterns of Fashion 1680–1860*, Wace & Co Ltd, 1964

BALLIN, ADA S., *Children's Dress*, for Council of International Health Exhibition by William Clowes & Sons, 1884
BALLIN, ADA S., *The Science of Dress*, Sampson Low, 1885
BRADFIELD, NANCY, *Costume in Detail 1730–1930*, Harrap, 1968
BROOKE, IRIS, *A History of English Costume*, Methuen, 1937
BROOKE, IRIS, *English Costume in the Seventeenth Century*, A. & C. Black 1954, reprinted 1958
BUCK, ANNE, *Victorian Costume & Costume Accessories*, Herbert Jenkins, 1961

Catalogue of Great Exhibition, 1851
Corsetry & Underwear, Circle Publications, 1935–1977
CUNNINGTON, C. WILLETT AND PHILLIS, *The History of Underclothes*, Michael Joseph, 1951
CUNNINGTON, PHILLIS AND MANSFIELD, ALAN, *English Costume for Sports and Outdoor Recreation. From the 16th to the 19th centuries*, A. & C. Black, 1969

DELANY, MRS, *Life and Letters*, 1746
DORNER, JANE, *The Changing Shape of Fashion*, Octopus Books, 1974
DOUGLAS, MRS F., *The Gentlewoman's Book of Dress*, Henry & Co, 1895
DUFF GORDON, LADY, *Discretions and Indiscretions*, Jarrolds, 1932

EVANS, DR JOAN, *Dress in Medieval France*, Oxford University Press, 1952

GARLAND, MADGE, *Fashion*, Penguin Books, 1962
GIBBS-SMITH, CHARLES H., *The Fashionable Lady in the 19th Century*, HM Stationery Office, 1960
GRASS, MILTON E., *History of Hosiery*, Fairchild Pubns, 1953

HAWEIS, MRS E., *The Art of Dress*, Chatto & Windus, 1879

In Our Own Fashion, Harley Publishing Company, 1956

JAEGER, GUSTAV, *Health Culture*, translated by Lewis R.S. Tomalin, new revised edition, Dr Jaeger's Sanitary Woollen System Co Ltd, 1907

LAVER, JAMES, *Concise History of Costume*, Thames & Hudson, 1969
LAVER, JAMES, *Fashion*, Cassell, 1963
LAVER, JAMES, *Modesty in Dress*, Heinemann, 1969
LIBRON F. AND CLOUZOT H., *Le Corset dans l'art et les moeurs du XIIIe au XXe siècles,* Paris, 1933
LIMNER, LUKE (JOHN LEIGHTON), *Madre Natura versus the Moloch of Fashion*, Chatto & Windus, 1874
LORD, WILLIAM BARRY, *The Corset and the Crinoline*, Ward Lock & Tyler, 1868

MERRIFIELD, MRS, *Dress as a Fine Art*, Arthur Hall, Virtue & Co, 1854
MOORE, DORIS LANGLEY, *The Woman in Fashion,* Batsford, 1949

NEWTON, STELLA MARY, *Health, Art and Reason*, J. Murray, 1974

PETRIE, SIR CHARLES, *Great Beginnings in the Age of Queen Victoria*, Macmillan, 1967
PLANCHE, J.R., *History of British Costume,* G. Bell 1834, 2nd Edition 1847
POIRET, PAUL, *My First Fifty Years*, Gollancz, 1934
PRITCHARD, MRS ERIC, *The Cult of Chiffon*, Grant Richards, 1902

QUENNELL, PETER, *Victorian Panorama*, Batsford, 1937

REES, GORONWY, *St. Michael*; *A History of Marks & Spencer,* Weidenfeld & Nicolson, 1969

ST. LAURENT, CECIL, *The History of Ladies' Underwear*, Michael Joseph, 1968

SAUNDERS, EDITH, *The Age of Worth*, Longmans Green, 1954

SIBBALD, SUSAN, *Memoirs of Susan Sibbald*, edited by Francis Paget Hett, Bodley Head, 1926

STANILAND, KAY, *The Medieval Corset, Costume Vol 3*, Costume Society, 1969

STRACHEY, RAY, *The Cause*, G. Bell, 1928

TAYLOR, JOHN, *It's a Small, Medium and Outsize World*, Hugh Evelyn, 1966

WAUGH, NORAH, *Corsets & Crinolines*, Batsford, 1954

WHITE, CYNTHIA L., *Women's Magazines 1693–1968*, Michael Joseph, 1970

WILCOX, R. TURNER, *The Mode in Costume*, Scribner's, 1947

WILCOX, R. TURNER, *The Dictionary of Costume*, Scribner's, 1969

YARWOOD, DOREEN, *English Costume*, Batsford, 1952, 3rd Edn 1973

YARWOOD, DOREEN, *European Costume*, Batsford, 1975

YOOLL, EMILY, *The History of the Corset*, Gossard, 1946

USA Bibliography

Adburgham, Alison. *View of Fashion*. Allen & Unwin, 1966.

Aglaia. John Heddon, 1893–4.

Allen, Agnes. *The Story of Clothes*. Faber & Faber, 1955.

Arnold, Janet. *Patterns of Fashion 1680–1860*. Macmillan Publishers, 1972; New York: Drama Book Specialists, 1972.

Ballin, Ada S. *Children's Dress*. For Council of International Health Exhibition by William Clowes & Sons. 1884.

Ballin, Ada S. *The Science of Dress*. Sampson Low, 1885.

Bradfield, Nancy. *Costume in Detail 1730–1930*. Harrap, 1968; Boston: Plays, 1968.

Brooke, Iris. *English Costume in the Seventeenth Century*. A. & C. Black, 1958; Atlantic Highlands, N.J.: Humanities Press, 1977.

Brooke, Iris. *A History of English Costume*. Methuen, 1937; New York: Theatre Arts Books, 1973.

Buck, Anne. *Victorian Costume & Costume Accessories*. Herbert Jenkins, 1961.

Catalogue of Great Exhibition, 1851.

Corsetry & Underwear. Circle Publications, 1935–1977.

Cunnington, C. Willett and Phillis. *The History of Underclothes*. Michael Joseph, 1951; New York: Gordon Press, 1976.

Cunnington, Phillis, and Mansfield, Alan. *English Costume for Sports and Outdoor Recreation; From the 16th to the 19th centuries*. A. & C. Black, 1969.

Delany, Mrs. *Life and Letters, 1746*.

Dorner, Jane. *The Changing Shape of Fashion*. Octopus Books, 1974.

Douglas, Mrs. F. *The Gentlewoman's Book of Dress*. Henry & Co., 1895.

Duff Gordon, Lady. *Discretions and Indiscretions*. Jarrolds, 1932.

Evans, Dr. Joan. *Dress in Medieval France*. Oxford University Press, 1952.

Garland, Madge. *Fashion*. Penguin Books, 1962.

Gibbs-Smith, Charles H. *The Fashionable Lady in the 19th Century*. H.M. Stationery Office, 1960.

Grass, Milton E. *History of Hosiery*. Fairchild Publications, 1953.

Haweis, Mrs. E. *The Art of Dress*. Chatto & Windus, 1879.

In Our Own Fashion. Harley Publishing Company, 1956.

Jaeger, Gustav. *Health Culture*. Translated by Lewis R.S. Tomalin. Dr. Jaeger's Sanitary Woollen System Co. Ltd., 1907.

Laver, James. *Concise History of Costume & Fashion*. Thames & Hudson, 1969; New York: Charles Scribner's Sons, 1974.

Laver, James. *Fashion*. Cassell, 1963.

Laver, James. *Modesty in Dress*. Heinemann, 1969.

Libron, F., and Clouzot, H. *Le Corset dans l'art et les moeurs du XIIIe au XXe siècles*. Paris, 1933.

Limner, Luke (John Leighton). *Madre Natura versus the Moloch of Fashion.* Chatto & Windus, 1874.

Lord, William Barry. *The Corset and the Crinoline.* Ward Lock & Tyler, 1868.

Merrifield, Mrs. *Dress as a Fine Art.* Arthur Hall, Virtue & Co., 1854.

Moore, Doris Langley, *The Woman in Fashion.* Batsford, 1949.

Newton, Stella Mary. *Health, Art and Reason.* J. Murray, 1974; New York: Abner Schram, 1976.

Petrie, Sir Charles. *Great Beginnings in the Age of Queen Victoria.* Macmillan Publishers, 1967.

Planché, J.R. *History of British Costume.* G. Bell, 1847.

Poiret, Paul. *My First Fifty Years.* Gollancz, 1934.

Pritchard, Mrs. Eric. *The Cult of Chiffon.* Grant Richards, 1902.

Quennell, Peter. *Victorian Panorama.* Batsford, 1937.

Rees, Goronwy. *St. Michael; A History of Marks & Spencer.* Weidenfeld & Nicolson, 1969.

St. Laurent, Cecil. *The History of Ladies' Underwear.* Michael Joseph, 1968.

Saunders, Edith. *The Age of Worth.* Longmans Green, 1954.

Sibbald, Susan. *Memoirs of Susan Sibbald.* Edited by Francis Paget Hett. Bodley Head, 1926.

Staniland, Kay. *The Medieval Corset. Costume Vol. 3.* Costume Society, 1969.

Strachey, Ray. *Cause: A History of the Women's Movement in Great Britain.* G. Bell, 1928; Port Washington, N.Y.: Kennikat Press, 1969.

Taylor, John. *It's a Small, Medium and Outsize World.* Hugh Evelyn, 1966.

Waugh, Norah. *Corsets & Crinolines.* Batsford, 1954; New York: Theatre Arts Books, 1954.

White, Cynthia L. *Women's Magazines 1693–1968.* Michael Joseph, 1970.

Wilcox, R. Turner. *The Dictionary of Costume.* Scribner's, 1969.

Wilcox, R. Turner. *The Mode in Costume.* Scribner's, 1947.

Yarwood, Doreen. *English Costume.* Batsford, 1973; Chester Springs, Pa.: Dufour Editions, 1953.

Yarwood, Doreen. *European Costume.* Batsford, 1975.

Yooll, Emily. *The History of the Corset.* Gossard, 1946.

Index

References to illustrations are shown in **bold type** by page numbers